Head Space and Timing:
Veteran Mental Health from a Combat Veteran Perspective

Duane K. L. France, MA, MBA, LPC

HEAD SPACE AND TIMING

Published By:
NCO Historical Society
P.O. Box 1341
Temple, TX 76503
www.ncohistory.com

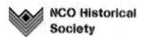

NCO Historical
Society

The content of this book has been previously published in a digital format on the Head Space and Timing blog, located at www.veteranmentalhealth.com

Cover Design by Extended Imagery

The author of this book is a Mental Health Counselor licensed to practice in the state of Colorado. The thoughts, ideas, musings, and posts in this book come from his military experience, professional experience, and personal opinions. They do NOT, however, represent professional advice. While he is a Mental Health Counselor, he is not YOUR Mental Health Counselor, and the guidance in this work should not be considered a substitute for working with a licensed clinical mental health provider. The opinions expressed here are his own, and in no way should be seen as reflection of his agency, his profession, or any professional associations that he is connected with.

ISBN: 0-9963181-4-3

ISBN-13: 978-0-9963181-4-3

Published in the United States of America

2nd Edition

To The Veterans Ward, El Paso County Jail.

It was for you to begin with.

Contents

Preface

In 2017, I was approached by a couple of incarcerated veterans looking for some support. At the time, I was working as a mental health counselor for the Colorado 4th Judicial District Veteran Trauma Court. We were making weekly visits to the county jail.

On any given day, the El Paso County Jail held 150-200 service members or veterans. In a community with as large a veteran population as Colorado Springs and the surrounding area, that may not be very surprising. On the other hand, the fact that these men and women served our country then ended up on the wrong side of the law is a tragedy and a shame.

The El Paso County Sheriff's Department, which had the responsibility for the administration of the jail, acknowledges the fact that a significant number of their population are veterans. In order to address this, a group of deputies…all veterans themselves…decided to create a Veterans Ward, a containment unit where incarcerated veterans were held with other veterans. With only 72 beds, it only supported about half of the veteran population in the jail, but it provided an opportunity for those who served to be housed together.

The Veterans Ward became a place for incarcerated veterans to support each other. To remind each other that they once served, honorably, and could regain some of the stability they had while they were in the military by re-discovering the values that made them successful.

In 2016, a group of incarcerated veterans formed a peer-led support group called Warriors First. The concept behind Warriors First was that veterans would follow a set schedule of groups designed to help them stay out of jail once they were released. To rediscover their Warrior Ethos and regain the pride of self that they had in the service.

The support that the veterans were looking for were articles focused on mental health and wellness, specifically for veterans. They wanted to model some of their programming off of Alcoholics Anonymous, in which the group would read a passage from the Big Book and there would be a discussion about the topics and concepts in the day's reading.

I provided a few articles that had been written for the Head Space and Timing Blog, which at that time had been going for just over a year. When I returned the next week, the veterans talked about how grateful they were, and how beneficial the group found the few articles I provided. Were there more that I could give them?

The book that you're reading now is the result of that request.

I collected the fifty-two most popular blog posts of 2016 and compiled them into a book that the Warriors First veterans could use. There was one article per week, designed to last the group the entire year.

As the time passed, the use of the collection of articles and the group expanded, both to veterans incarcerated in the Colorado penal system, and to Warriors First groups in the community. The feedback from these original veterans remains strong, and I was encouraged to release the collection to a wider audience.

It's necessary to understand that, on any given night, there are a number of veterans struggling to survive. They're incarcerated. They're homeless. They've served, and many times, the nature of that service caused them to fail to readjust to society. If you served in the military, perhaps something in this book can help you develop some awareness around some of the struggles and problems you've had in post military life. If youre the family member of someone who is serving or has served, maybe this will help you understand more about what your service member experienced. And if you are someone in the community who is looking to support veterans, like a case manager, social worker, or mental health professional, maybe this book will be a tool and a guide for you to develop some awareness about how to help.

Because serving those who served is the responsibility of all who values the freedom won by the sacrifice of our service members, past, present and future.

A final note, an explanation of the title of this book, the blog found at www.veteranmentalhealth.com, and the Head Space and Timing podcast. The Browning M2 Machine Gun, also known as the .50 Cal, is a weapon that has been used in nearly every branch of the military on many different platforms: mounted to vehicles, ships, boats, aircraft, and helicopters. This weapon is durable, dependable, and strong. Many of these weapons were manufactured in the '50s and '60s. You can drop 'em, smack 'em, submerse them in dust and grit, and still they will fire.

Unless you don't get the headspace and timing set right.

With this weapon, the service member must ensure that the headspace, the distance between the face of the bolt and the chamber, is properly set, and that the timing ensures that the round fires at the appropriate time. The weapon itself is huge…the overall length is over 5 feet. The headspace and timing gauge…about the size of your thumb.

I consider veterans to be resilient, capable, strong. You can drop 'em, you can smack 'em, submerse them in dust, grit, fire, water, the sun and the snow, and still they'll come back at you.

Unless they don't have their own head space and timing set right.

If one of the greatest weapons in the military's arsenal needs adjustment every now and then to operate properly, then why would we consider the operator of that weapon to be any different?

Duane K. L. France, MA, MBA, LPC

21 May 2109

THE MISSION IS THE WELFARE OF THE SOLDIER

The Army's Creed of the Noncommissioned Officer[1] contains these critical lines:

"My two basic responsibilities will always be uppermost in my mind: the accomplishment of my mission and the welfare of my Soldiers."

Those two points of focus encapsulated everything that I was as a leader: the mission I was required to accomplish and the welfare of those who trusted me to lead them. Once I retired from the Army, however, the focus didn't change…but now, the mission is the welfare of the Soldier, Sailor, Airman, Marine, and Coast Guardsman.

Veterans need your help. Not the kind of help that comes with a new license plate, or stickers on a window, or even a sincere "thank you for your service." All of those things are great, and necessary, for both you and the veteran. But they are not what the veteran needs.

I have found that a veteran needs to feel safe. Wants to feel normal. Needs to understand that the things they experienced, what they went through, did not "warp" them or "corrupt" them. Veterans need to understand that they are not "crazy".

I am a veteran myself, over 22 years in the Army with three combat tours and several additional operational deployments. This is not about me, though, not some shameless self-promotion geared towards greater visibility. This is about lending weight and legitimacy to what I have to say…I know whereof I speak, in a sense.

I am also a mental health counselor, and currently work with veterans involved in the justice system. They have made mistakes, like the rest of us. They need my help. They need YOUR help. They need to know, as they have left the military for whatever reason, that the simple act of raising their hand and swearing to support and defend the constitution of the United States was a turning point in their life.

What follows is a compilation of my thoughts on different aspects of veteran life, mental health, and wellness. If we run into each other, let's talk about the stigma that exists that keeps veterans from talking about their fears, their triumphs, their disappointments, and their grief. Let's talk about what we can do to satisfy the needs that veterans have.

Let's truly help veterans, one at a time, understand that their welfare is our mission.

AN OPEN LETTER TO AMERICA, FROM ONE OF YOUR VETERANS

Dear America,

Just wanted to take a few minutes to say thanks and get a few things off my chest. Life's been a little challenging for us veterans, maybe more than we expected.

When I joined your Armed Forces, I looked around and saw a cross-section of your citizens that I never knew existed before. The brothers and sisters that I saw while I was in came from every state, every ethnicity, and every religion. I saw a Caucasian from California become best friends with an African-American from Mississippi. I didn't think much of it at the time, but looking back on it, that was kind of amazing, you know? See, when we banded together for a common goal, where a person was from, what they liked or didn't like, it didn't seem to matter as much as whether or not that person could get things done. Sometimes I wonder, why can't the rest of your communities be like that?

My reasons for joining your military were as widely different from those of my fellow service members as where we came from. To be honest, life wasn't always so hot growing up, and maybe joining the service was my only choice to make and the best thing that happened to me, all at the same time. I saw brothers and sisters who joined to pay for college, and then never ended up going to college. My fellow veterans joined because they loved you, because they wanted to get out of where they were at, or because they came from a military family. Once we joined, though, we learned the values of our particular branch of service, and pretty much came to have them as our own: Loyalty. Integrity. Selfless Service. Let me tell you, once you start to believe in stuff like that, it's really hard to un-believe it. When you do stop believing in those things, it leaves you in a cold place. It's hard to come back to civilian life and not see those things in the people around me who never served.

I grew up watching how veterans from my parent's generation were treated, and how veterans from my grandparent's generation were treated. I thank them for their service and sacrifice, but why was it so different for each of them? Things change, I get it, but come on! To have veterans of WWII revered, Korean War veterans forgotten, Vietnam veterans reviled, and Gulf War veterans forgotten again…really? They joined your military, just like I did. Are we going to keep the cycle going? How will your people see me and my brothers and sisters in fifty years? If how I see things going now is any indication, it's probably going to be a mix of all of them!

Do you know why I love you so much? Because I saw firsthand what it was like to live in a place that was NOT you. Some of it looked like it really sucked, to put it mildly, and I couldn't wait to get back to you. They say that you don't really appreciate something until you don't have it anymore, and that's certainly true; your military sent me to places that really opened my eyes on that point. There were some really great places, and I thank you for sending me to them; there were also some really crappy places, and it's harder for me to thank you for sending me there. What I do thank you for is sending me to those crappy places with my brothers and sisters…that made it a whole heck of a lot easier.

Your leaders sent me to combat, but I don't really hold that against them. I know what I signed up for, and if I didn't, I figured it out pretty quick. It didn't much matter which political party was in charge, I seemed to get sent to someplace where someone shot at me, so who was in the White House didn't bother me all that much. It's not that I'm not interested in politics…I kind of really am, to tell you the truth, because my job was very much an extreme extension of politics…but who my Senator was seemed to matter a whole heck of a lot less than who my Battle Buddy was. I was somewhat more concerned about who was playing in the World Series or the National Championship than which laws were being passed in Congress. I know I can't speak for all of my brothers and sisters, but it seemed like there were a lot more important things that were going on, and sometimes I just needed a break. That being said, though, I would appreciate some assistance on the legislative front, even if it is making sure that things are in place so I can receive what I was promised when I joined your military.

So I guess the reason I'm writing this letter to you, America, is to kind of let you know where I'm coming from, and to ask for a few favors.

Just give me a shot at the American Dream. I don't want the nice house, good job, peaceful life served up to me on a platter. I wouldn't feel like I've earned it if you just give it to me, and I'm used to working for what I get. I don't want a handout, but I also don't want to be left out in the cold…literally. While I love your cities and towns, I don't love them so much that I want to live on their streets all the time. While I love the idea of justice and fairness, sometimes it's hard for me to readjust from how I had to think when I was overseas to how I know I need to think here at home, and experiencing fairness and justice from behind bars just adds more challenges on top of what I'm already having. To be honest, I didn't really brush up on my interview skills, or resume writing, because I was kind of too busy doing the other stuff you needed me to do. So all I'm asking for is a little bit of consideration.

Don't let my fellow citizens treat me like a scared rabbit or wounded bird, or worse, like a rabid animal that everyone needs to run away from. Being coddled or marginalized would irritate the crap out of anybody, but it burns me up particularly. My experiences don't define me, and the Purple Hearts, traumatic brain injury, and mental health diagnoses of my brothers and sisters don't define them. I want to survive, and thrive, in spite of what I did and what happened to me, and not because of what I did and what happened. I really do need help sometimes, real concrete help in the form of medical services and mental health services, not in the form of another fishing license or commemorative license plate. But just because I need help sometimes, and it's hard to ask for that help, doesn't mean that I am a crazy combat vet or system-dependent leech on the taxpayer's dime. It means some of the stuff that happened screwed me up, and I might need some help getting unscrewed up.

So thanks, America, for taking the time to hear me out. I love you, and wouldn't want to be from anywhere else. I'd just like the opportunity to have my life and my family's life be just a little bit easier than it was in the past, and if there's any way you could help make that happen, I'd certainly appreciate it.

Yours truly, A Veteran

A VETERAN NAMED SKIP AND HIS STRUGGLE WITH PTSD

Skip wasn't the same when he came back from the war. By many accounts, including his own, he was a pretty "good boy" growing up, active in his community, doing well in school. It wasn't easy growing up in Detroit, he didn't know his biological father, but he and his younger half-brother were raised well by his mother. When he got back, though, things seemed to change.

Those who knew him before didn't know about the nightmares. Those who were closest to him were allowed to see the pictures, though, pictures of his time overseas. Some of them were pictures of the enemy dead. He had a hard time getting a job; although he was previously outgoing and friendly, he didn't have much success in job interviews. He only tried to apply for low-level jobs with minimal qualifications, and still struggled. When asked questions by prospective employers, he would mumble, and wouldn't get the job.

After a while, though, he did land a good job. He got it based on his veteran status, because of what happened while he deployed. Things really seemed like they were turning around. He got married, and he and his new wife moved into a house in a better part of Detroit. He couldn't quite afford it on what he was being paid, but he thought it was something that they should have. His good humor started to come back, he and his wife had a son, and he started to become more active in his community again.

Slowly, though, things started to unravel. The bills were starting to pile up. Skip bounced a check at the grocery store, but he was still picking up the tab wherever he went, running up the family's credit card. He didn't talk about his time during the war; one of the few who knew some of what happened was his wife, and she only knew because she slept in the same bed. She found out fairly quickly that she should wake him up from the other side of the room, because he could be dangerous when she woke him up abruptly.

He started missing important meetings at work. The police were called one night, because he threatened to shoot his neighbors because of their barking dog. He started experiencing stomach pains and was diagnosed with ulcers…and finally referred to mental health. When he finally did start to talk to someone about the stuff that happened while he was deployed, it didn't go well; he was in and out of inpatient facilities over a period of eighteen months. There were times that he would engage with his treatment providers, talking about what happened, the vivid memories that had haunted him for over two years, and then there were times that he would take off.

He finally left treatment for good. His car was repossessed, so he used some back pay and bought another one. He took out a loan that he wouldn't be able to repay, and stayed at home and slept or watched TV. He had not paid his mortgage in nine months, his wife was in the hospital for a surgical procedure that he couldn't afford, and the house was about to be foreclosed.

One night, Skip called a friend and asked them to give him a ride to see someone who would help him out with some money. After catching a ride from his friend, Skip went to a bar, had a couple of drinks, and then walked across the street to a convenience store.

Skip walked up to the register to buy a pack of cigarettes; when the cashier opened the register, Skip pulled out a .22 caliber pistol and demanded the cash. There was a struggle for Skip's gun, and he pulled the trigger, twice, wounding the cashier…then the cashier, the owner of the convenience store, reached down for his own gun and opened fire on Skip. The owner warned Skip, even after shooting him twice, that he was going to kill him, but Skip didn't move, and didn't stop pointing his gun…so the owner continued to fire.

Skip was taken to the hospital and pronounced dead. His funeral was held with full military honors at Arlington National Cemetery, and he currently rests in Lot 471, Section 31.

Sound familiar? It might, but not for the reasons you might think. Dwight "Skip" Johnson was a veteran of the Vietnam War, and was awarded the Congressional Medal of Honor for his actions in a battle near Dak To on January 14, 1968[1] .

This story was deliberately told backwards, and out of sync. There is much more to Dwight's story than what I wrote here, but the similarities between his experiences and the experiences of veterans today are striking. Even the circumstances the firefight that resulted in his Medal of Honor are familiar to many veterans today: after spending a year as a member of a tank crew that he grew to love as a family, he was inexplicably switched to another tank crew the day before the battle at Dak To. His old tank took a direct hit in the opening moments of the battle, and Dwight…Skip…became overwhelmed with rage and grief. This happens so frequently, and tragically, that it's one of the most common stories with veterans who struggle with unresolved grief. They're usually the gunner on one truck, and they are pulled to be a driver on another; then their old truck gets hit. One Soldier is kept back off of a mission for some reason, and the one who replaces them is killed.

Dwight's story played out a full decade before Posttraumatic Stress Disorder was recognized as a psychological condition, and similar stories are playing out today, three decades after PTSD became a thing. There has been progress, and relief is possible, even though PTSD does not fully explain all of Dwight's challenges.

I first read about Specialist Johnson's life and tragic death in the book, Medal of Honor: Profiles of America's Military Heroes From the Civil War to the Present by Allen Mikaelian. A significant portion of this article was based on his profile from this book, and his story certainly warrants a deeper read. If you are a veteran, are the family member of a veteran, or work with veterans in any way, this book is an excellent resource for a look at what veterans experience.

One of the most poignant statements made about Skip's life came from his mother, which was chosen to end an article that was written about him in 1971[2], and chosen to end his profile in the Medal of Honor book: "Sometimes I wonder if Skip tired of this life and needed someone else to pull the trigger."

Sound familiar? Hopefully not. But it probably does. If you're a veteran, reach out for help. If you're a family member and you see something familiar here, reach out for help as well. One tragic ending like Dwight Johnson is enough for this world.

WE LOST ANOTHER VETERAN YESTERDAY

I don't know who they were, but they odds are nearly 100% perfect that it's true. It will be true on the day I write this, and it will be true on the day that you read it. Another Veteran will have succumbed to the struggle and died by suicide.

The Veteran who took their own life yesterday does not fit any specific set of criteria. There are no biases, no discrimination when it comes to the epidemic of suicide. She could have been a young female OIF/OEF Veteran; he could be an older male Vietnam Veteran. The despair knows no boundaries, plays by no rules, picks no favorites. It attacks grandparents, sons, daughters, aunts, cousins, friends, lovers, strangers. This tragedy is not even bound by borders; Canada, the UK, countries around the world are struggling with increased suicide rates among veterans. The Veteran who took their life yesterday could have been someone from a coalition partner that we served with in Iraq or Afghanistan.

Rank or profession is not a protective factor. The Veteran who took their life yesterday could have been a senior leader, or a junior soldier; they could have had all the resources in the world, or no resources at all. This insidious event has taken Chaplains, mental health professionals, medical professionals. All Veterans. All vulnerable, hurting, in pain.

Suicide, at it's most basic, is an attempt to stop pain: physical pain, emotional pain, even spiritual pain. But pain does not last forever; suicide does.

As time continues to pass, many among us realize that we have lost more friends after deployment than we did during deployment. For those of you who served, you understand what I'm talking about, and understand how impactful that is; many units suffered significant casualties while deployed, enough for a lifetime. But the losses by suicide eclipse those; even one Veteran death by suicide is enough for a lifetime. It is my prayer that the loss yesterday is the last, because I so desperately want this to stop, but I understand that it will likely not.

There have been small conversations about this, and giant multi-series articles about it. And it still happens. The thing about the Elephant in the Room is, even when we start talking about it, the Elephant is still there. Because it's huge. And real. Organizations such as #22Kill[1] and the IAVA[2] have made efforts to talk about it; there are national hotlines and state hotlines available for those in need, there are technologies such as the Objective Zero[3] app, there are countless websites, blogs, chats, groups, organizations, foundations, and nonprofits dedicated to putting a stop to this detestable event. And yet it still happens.

But that's where you come in.

Because yesterday, a Veteran's life was saved. Someone reached out at just the right time. Someone said just the right thing that was needed at the exact moment that was needed…and that's how we take care of the Elephant in the Room. Remember the old saying? How do you eat an elephant? Pick and ear and start chewing.

You. Right there, reading this. You have the ability to save a veteran's life. I know you have the desire. Keep an eye out for the opportunity.

You may wonder, "What can I do?" The answer is: simply be present. Show up to the fight. Reach out to your old Veteran buddies, let them know that you are there if they need it. Let them know that you will answer the phone, day or night, rainstorm or snowstorm, close or far away. You don't know what to say…that's fine. There have been times where others have told me that something I said helped them out of a dark place, and I didn't even know they were struggling at the time.

You and I, individually, are not going to keep every Veteran from taking their own life tomorrow; the #22Kill ring that I have on my finger is not some magic talisman that is going to somehow infuse me with the mystic power of suicide prevention. What that ring does, however, is keep my goal in my mind. When I look at it, I am consciously reminded that I must be aware of the signs of hopelessness and despair in those Veterans I come across…whenever or wherever I meet them, if it is sitting in front of me in my office, in jail, online. I don't want to see another individual who has served their country to die. I don't want to see them homeless. I don't want to see them behind bars.

You have the ability to save a Veteran's life tomorrow. You don't have to be a Veteran to do so, but many who served feel that only another Veteran will understand. If you sense that someone is hurting, then reach out. Ask them. Let them know that whatever hopeless and despairing place they may be in, they are not alone. Coming from a complete stranger, that could mean next to nothing; coming from someone they served with, that could mean everything. Put your hand on their shoulder, look them in the eye, and tell them, "Seriously. Dude. I don't want you to die." Easy? No. But neither was reading this post. Neither is reading the articles. Neither is realizing that, unless I do something with those in my immediate circle of trust, this tragedy will not end.

If you are hurting, reach out. If someone sent this to you, then they care enough to let you know that they want you to live. Is asking for help easy? Sometimes, yes. Many times, no. Do you feel like no one understands? Sure, but just because you think nobody cares or understands doesn't make it true. The fact is that even if there is one person who does not want to see you die, then there is someone in the world who cares. If there is one, then the hope is that there will be more. With hope, and with help, the veteran's life that can be saved tomorrow can be yours.

I searched for "veteran suicide prevention" on Google and came up with 547,000 results in .3 seconds. The resources are out there...but the greatest resource in this fight is one person reaching out to another. Together, we can get the elephant out of the room.

A MESSAGE FROM A VETERAN TO VETERANS: YOU HAVE THE POTENTIAL TO CHANGE THE WORLD

Maybe you already know this. Maybe you're already working towards making this happen.

Then again, maybe you're not.

I had three sets of grandparents. What can I say, benefits of the modern blended family. All three of my grandmothers were sweet and loving, my grandfathers caring in their own unique and different ways. Two of them served in the military during World War II.

I was having a conversation with one of them…this was after I joined the Army, mind you, so I was in my twenties…and he was telling me of a time when he and a bunch of his buddies were messing around in France changing around the signs that pointed to different villages…I said, "wait…What? You were in France during WWII?" He smiled, said he didn't talk about it much, focused on the funny stuff rather than anything else.

We are often reminded of the impact of the World War II generation on America. In 1998, Tom Brokaw[1] wrote, "The Greatest Generation," a book about how those veterans returned to a country and did stuff. They made things happen. They became lawmakers, celebrities, lawyers, entrepreneurs. They also, like my grandfathers, became tailors and mechanics. They built lives around the things that they loved, and, in doing so, changed the world.

The world, our nation, was different then, seventy-five years ago. When the service members left to fight the war, it impacted nearly every aspect of the country. The service that was being provided overseas was equaled by the service that was provided here; factories, industry was kept going by the labor of the hands of the mothers, wives, and daughters of those service members.

Things are, of course, different now. One of the possible reasons that the WWII generation had such an impact was that it was impossible not to: according to the Department of Veterans Affairs[2], over 16 million veterans served in WWII. That is compared to 1.7 million theater deployed service members to the Korean War, 3.4 million deployed to Southeast Asia, and just under 700,000 deployed to Desert Shield/Desert Storm.

According to the same source, there are 4.3 million veterans of the Global War on Terror. We number just over a quarter of the veterans that served in World War II, but GWOT veterans comprise the largest number of combat veterans in seventy-five years.

We have to make that count for something.

Yes, our world is changed. The veteran is increasingly isolated, returning to civilian life surrounded by a community that is likely unaware that there is still a war going on. As a country, we don't have the sense of a common bond forged by overcoming a common hardship. Our numbers are less than our veterans of previous generations, but we have an advantage that they didn't have. Because of their sacrifice and hard work, because of their effort, we now have the technology and the opportunities that we have to make significant changes.

I firmly believe that we have the opportunity, even the responsibility, to become the next Greatest Generation.

"No one gives a crap about veterans unless it's Memorial Day or Veteran's Day." Any time I hear of an absolute, I question the intent behind the statement…no one? Really? Not true. Maybe it's based on our own personal experiences, but let's say that there are a large number of people in this country that may not be as familiar with, or don't care about, veterans. Okay. But when I was in the Army, I didn't ask for anyone else to take care of the Soldiers I was responsible for; I did it. If another Platoon Sergeant came to me and said, "Hey, I took care of one of your guys who needed help," I would have been pissed. So look at it now the same way. So what if someone else doesn't care about veterans. VETERANS care about veterans, so we'll take care of our own. And that starts with taking care of ourselves.

So current era veterans, along with our veteran brothers and sisters from Vietnam, the Cold War, and the Gulf War, have the ability to make some significant impacts. We are branching out into the Tech field. Veterans are in significant positions at Amazon, LinkedIn, Microsoft, Google, name the company, find a vet. We are becoming teachers; at my kid's school, a charter school system governed by a 501(c)3 nonprofit, teachers are veterans. Administrators are veterans, or spouses of veterans. Over half of the members of the Board of Directors are veterans. Veterans are being elected to city, state, and federal government. I don't care what side of the aisle you sit on…the fact that you're a veteran is important.

We have an opportunity. Now. Today. Moving towards the future. We can get out of our own heads, leave the sense of entitlement at the door, and move forward without the righteous indignation and start to make something of our country and ourselves.

Let's fulfill the oath that we gave when we enlisted or commissioned into the military. No, I'm not talking about the part about the Uniformed Code of Military Justice, or the superiors appointed over me. I'm talking about supporting and defending. Bearing true faith and allegiance.

I'm talking about becoming the leaders, the doers, the fathers and mothers, the supporters of our families.

I'm talking about creating a future. If not us, then who…if not now, then when?

LESSONS FROM A POW ON RESILIENCE, PERSEVERANCE, AND VETERAN MENTAL HEALTH

If you want to see an example of military resilience, take a look at the movie Unbroken[1]. This is a dramatization of the true story of Louis Zamperini, the Olympic athlete, Army Air Corps Bombardier, and WWII POW.

The lessons in Louis' life are significant and many. Perseverance. Resilience. Sheer unstoppable will. One of the key moments in the film that struck me, however, was an exchange that Zamperini had with a fellow POW. He had endured significant torture and abuse, some beyond even what his fellow POWs experienced, and was feeling disheartened and discouraged. He expressed hatred and determination to his fellow prisoner, and committed to beating the captor who was tormenting him. In response, Louis was told:

We can beat them by making it to the end of the war alive.

We can win by endurance. Sheer force of will. The idea of, "if I can take it, I can make it" became Zamperini's talismanic phrase that helped him endure horrendous torture.

As inspiring as Zamperini's story is, I was reminded of another phrase from a different medium, Paul Dillon's interview by Byron Chen on the SuccessVets podcast[2]. Dillon is describing the differences between his return from Vietnam compared to how returning veterans today are greeted, and says something to the effect of:

We have finally been able to separate the war from the warrior

The key words that both of these phrases have in common is: the war. Combat. In its many forms, through generations of conflicts, across the landscape of many nations. For many, the war ended the moment they returned home, in one sense; however, for many, the war continues, only in the battlefield of their minds instead of the land of foreign countries.

When I heard those two phrases separately, I thought to myself each time…they could be talking about veteran mental health.

We can overcome our challenges…our war…with depression, anxiety, substance addiction, and posttraumatic stress disorder by making it to the end of the war alive. By any honorable, beneficial, and appropriate means necessary. By not allowing the memories of the past to put a stranglehold on to our present and hold our future hostage, by not allowing ourselves to succumb to negative perceptions about ourselves and others. By not allowing the depression to overwhelm us to the point where we take our own lives, not allowing the anxiety to hobble us to the point where our lives are lived isolated in dark rooms. Not every veteran struggles with mental health concerns after returning from combat, but a significant number do, and they are still at war in their minds. At war with themselves. With their thoughts and emotions. With their family, friends, and communities, who at times feel like the closest allies and other times feel like the bitterest enemies. This is too often the war of the combat veteran, and, as Zamperini's fellow prisoner stated, we can beat these challenges by making it to the end of the war alive. By learning to endure, by reaching out for help, by figuring out some other way to manage our emotions rather than out of control rage or desensitization by substances, prescribed or otherwise.

Too often, veterans feel as though others don't understand them. Only those who have "been there" really "get it," and trying to help them to understand is an exercise in futility. Even worse, the war seemed to have gotten inside some veterans and festered, holding them hostage; the veteran themselves cannot separate the war from the warrior. If, in this context, the "war" is the struggle with the mental health challenges that some veterans experience when the return, then veterans begin to think that their mental health diagnoses define them. The war…depression, anxiety, substance use, PTSD…becomes the mark of the warrior, the price the warrior paid for their sacrifice.

While, as Dillon points out, the community has been successful at separating the war from the warrior, that applies to the two most recent conflicts, the wars in Iraq and Afghanistan. Although the conflicts themselves were not popular (or often even remembered), the public has been able to recognize that the warriors executing the combat actions were not synonymous with the war itself. Is that true if we consider the mental health challenges of the war in the same context? How many employers, concerned that a combat veteran may have PTSD or some other service related mental health concern, and choose not to hire them? It's not like a candidate's mental health can legally be a subject in a job interview, so if the hiring manager has the assumption that this is the case, then they have certainly not separated the war from the warrior. Not only does the veteran fail to separate the war from themselves as the warrior, in a very real sense, the unaware public does as well.

This can be overcome by awareness. By not allowing the battles to overcome us, to destroy us.

By separating the war from the warrior, and making it to the end of the war alive.

AWARENESS IS THE KEY TO RECOVERY FOR VETERANS

In my experience in working with veterans, I have come to understand that awareness is the key to healing and recovery. Awareness on the part of the veteran themselves, awareness on the part of the veteran's support network, and awareness on the part of the community.

The veteran themselves must become self-aware. We need to develop awareness that we are having difficulty adjusting to the transition from combat to garrison, difficulty adjusting to the transition from the military to civilian life. Second, we must develop awareness that there is nothing wrong with that difficulty…it is 100% normal, and even to be expected. Veterans also need to be aware that there are resources that can help them manage those difficulties, and that those resources actually work.

The veteran's support network also needs to be aware of the change that has occurred. The support network includes immediate family, such as spouse, children, parents, and siblings, as well as extended family and the veteran's social network…classmates, coworkers, friends. The people in these support networks need to be aware that the veteran they know is different from the veteran they knew…deployed or not, witnessed combat or not, struggling or not. When someone joins the military, they immerse themselves into a different culture. This is a lifestyle change, one that comes with it's own language, expected standards of conduct, and both written and unwritten rules. Once someone assimilates into that culture, grows to appreciate and even "love" it, then they are exposed to traumatic events, they are forever and irrevocably changed. I didn't say "broken" or "damaged" or "screwed up"…they are changed. We grow, we mature, daily we become the sum total of our experience in our life up to that point. Many in a veteran's support network want the veteran to be the "way they were", rather than accept how they are.

Finally, the community must become aware that this change occurs, in individual veterans themselves and in the population of veterans as a whole. The community needs to understand that the concept of "crazy combat vet" is not an image that veterans relish; not every veteran is John Rambo in First Blood, walking through life in a haze of flashbacks getting ready to lob pine cones as if they were hand grenades. Veterans want what everyone else wants; the opportunity to live a life worth living. To participate in meaningful work. To take care of and protect the ones they love. To continue to serve their community, but in their own way, and at their own pace. As a community, supporting a veteran takes the awareness that the image of "veteran" is more than just some anxiety-ridden, flashback-enduring hollow shell of a person. Enough veterans see themselves in this way…getting that image confirmed when they look in someone's eye just solidifies their image of themselves.

It is only when veterans, their families, and their communities come to this awareness that real change can start to happen. .

VIEW OF A VETERAN: I'M NO HERO, AND I'M NOT SPECIAL

Get any three veterans together in a room, and you're in for a lively conversation. Ask who is the strongest, fastest, and smartest, and you will get a variety of responses. Often, each will argue that they should be considered for the title.

Ask which of them is the bravest, the most heroic, and our three veterans will point at the other two, but not themselves. I will be the first to tell you that I'm no one special, that all I ever did was take care of my Soldiers, take care of my mission, and do the best that I could.

Talk to any veteran about their time in combat, and you will eventually get to the point where they say, "Well, as bad as I had it, at least I wasn't in…" At least I wasn't in the Korengal. Talk to veterans who were in the Korengal, however, and they say, "at least I wasn't at Keating." I would imagine that guys from Keating would say, "at least I wasn't in Ramadi," veterans of Ramadi saying, "at least I wasn't in Fallujah,' veterans of Fallujah saying, "at least I wasn't in the invasion," on and on, with each veteran knowing that someone, somewhere, had it worse than they did. OIF/OEF veterans point to the Vietnam days, saying, "Those guys had it rough", Vietnam guys point to Korea, back through American military history. The fact that someone else had it worse made it mean that that other vet was more of a hero than they were, were more worthy of honor and respect than they were. In many cases, that's true.

At Fort Bragg, there is an annual event called All American Week[1]. It's a huge reunion for former members of the 82nd Airborne Division, and there are events throughout the week. After a jump one day, a group of my Soldiers and I were meeting with some former paratroopers, and one of the old gentlemen asked one of my Soldiers, "how many jumps do you have, son?" My guy, proud as only an Airborne Soldier can be, puffs up his chest and says, "Nine!" The old paratrooper says, "Well, you sure have me beat, I only have three." "Three? That's it?" "Yeah, just the three…Normandy, Holland, and Sicily." It took my guy a minute to realize that he was talking about THE Normandy, Holland and Sicily, not just the drop zones on Bragg. In my book, that old paratrooper is a hero…but I'm sure he doesn't think so.

The fact is, simply serving in the military is a rare thing. In 2010, the U.S. Census[2] indicates that there are 21.8 million veterans living in America. That same census counted 308.7 million Americans; that comes to approximately 7%. If we accept the definition of "special" in its adjective form as something that is better, greater, or otherwise different from the usual, this statistic certainly fits that criteria. Even as I write this, however, something within me balks at the idea of describing myself as "better" or "greater".

When it comes to the real stuff, the important stuff, rarely will you get a veteran who has actually experienced combat describe themselves as a hero. It's not that they despise that designation…each will tell you that they know true heroes…but each will deny that they themselves deserve that designation. They will tell of one of their buddies who saved their life. They will tell of some squad leader who made a quick decision that resulted in success rather than failure. They will tell you that the true hero is the one that didn't make it back. Viktor Frankl, in Man's Search for Meaning[3] described concentration camp survivors in this way: "We who have come back, by the aid of many lucky chances or miracles – whatever one may choose to call them – we know: the best of us did not return." When I read those words, I understood them, in the most fundamental way that one can when someone puts into words the unspoken feeling inside them.

I once knew an NCO who had the opportunity to play an extra on the film, We Were Soldiers[4]. We didn't really believe him, until we all watched the movie and he paused it right at the scene where you could see his face…15 milliseconds of fame, and all that. He told a pretty cool story, though.

Lieutenant General Hal Moore was on the set as an advisor, and they were filming the scene where Mel Gibson is speaking to the troops before they shipped off to Vietnam. As they were watching the speech and Gibson said, "I will be the first to set foot on the field, and I will be the last to step off, and I will leave no one behind…dead or alive, we will all come home together," my buddy said he looked over at Hal Moore and saw tears streaming down his face. Later, a group of them were listening to him talk, and Lt. Gen. Moore said that those words affected him deeply, because there were Soldiers left behind. Not in the Ia Drang campaign, but in Vietnam…and they were often the best of them. Lt. Gen. Moore would claim that he's no hero.

If you're a veteran, I get it, no amount of convincing is going to make you feel like you did anything special. You're going to avoid claiming any service connected disability because "others deserve it more than I do." You're going to downplay your accomplishments because you didn't do what you did for the glory, and you certainly didn't do it for the pay. When anyone asks, you give them the old Joe Friday line from Dragnet: "Just doing my job, Ma'am."

The truth is, though, although you may not be a hero, and you may not be special, you have done some pretty heroic and special things. If you're not a veteran, maybe that will be helpful to remember as well.

PTSD: WHAT IT IS (AND WHAT IT ISN'T)

There has been much discussion regarding Posttraumatic Stress Disorder[1] in Veterans in the past thirty years, and rightly so. It is a very real condition that has a significant impact on the daily life of veterans, their families, and the community. There are some misconceptions about PTSD, however; it has become so widely known that much of society believes that any veteran who has been to combat has PTSD. Perhaps the following information will help to increase your awareness of what PTSD is…and what it isn't.

PTSD goes beyond the natural reaction to a traumatic event, and requires a very specific set of circumstances in order to meet the diagnostic criteria for the disorder. The veteran must be demonstrating behaviors related to four separate areas: intrusion, avoidance, negative alterations in thoughts and emotions, and alterations in arousal and reactions. The specific criteria listed in the Diagnostic and Statistical Manual for Mental Disorders, 5th Edition (DSM-5)[2] are:

A stressor must be present. The veteran must have been exposed to death, threatened death, serious injury, or sexual violence. They must have experienced it directly, witnessed it, heard about it happening to a close friend in clear detail, or have been repeatedly exposed to the results of traumatic events in the course of their duties. This does not need to have happened in combat; military service members who were deployed to New Orleans in response to Hurricane Katrina were required to recover flood victims, and have struggled with recovery. While deployed to Iraq, my unit had the responsibility of recovering battle-damaged vehicles, to include recovering their fellow Soldiers. One young Soldier who had this task, by the time we reached the halfway point of our deployment, had recovered more human remains than he had years on this earth. That is another aspect that makes PTSD in veterans unique: it is a result of not just one traumatic event, but a series of traumatic events over a deployment, or over several deployments.

Second, the veteran must persistently re-experience the traumatic event. This includes unwanted intrusive memories, nightmares, dissociating or "zoning out", experiencing distress after exposure to reminders of the event, or having an obvious physical reaction after exposure to something that reminds them of the trauma. These triggers can, and often do, include those things that people expect: loud heavy noises that remind a veteran of an explosive blast, quick sharp noises that remind us of gunfire, or large crowds of people. These can also include things that are not expected. The full moon, for example; when a veteran was out on patrol in combat, it was highly unlikely that the enemy had night vision capability. Therefore, when the full moon was out and the night was brighter, there was greater danger.

29

Turning that response off when we let the dogs out in the morning is very difficult. Smells, such as barbequing, or events, like stopping at a stoplight, or even something as seemingly innocuous as the shadows of clouds on a mountainside can cause a veteran to start to think about their combat experiences.

Third, the veteran must experience purposeful avoidance of the things that cause these reactions. We stop going places and doing things that remind us of our experiences. The veteran who experienced multiple IED attacks may stop driving altogether. They may stop going to family gatherings and concerts, even if they enjoyed doing those things prior to experiencing combat. Celebrating the Fourth of July is not even an option! This purposeful avoidance also leads to the veteran engaging in activities that numb their reactions…substance use, for example. Anything to avoid feeling what they're feeling.

Fourth, the veteran must experience negative changes in their thoughts and their moods. They think bad things about themselves: I am to blame for what happened, I am a monster for the things I did. They think bad things about the world: I am not safe here, no one can understand what I did. They experience diminished interest in things that pleased them before. They feel alienated, cut off, misunderstood, and experience an inability to feel positive emotions. The difficult thing with these thoughts is, once the veteran starts to think this way, they avoid any type of activity that could disprove those thoughts.

The veteran must also experience behavioral changes. Increasingly irritable or aggressive behavior, self-destructive or reckless behavior, hypervigilance, exaggerated startle response, difficulty concentrating or sleeping: these are all changes in behavior that veterans commonly experience. Many of us, upon return from combat, are seeking to continue to experience the thrill that we got while deployed; if we are not able to, then we get frustrated, irritable, angry.

These symptoms must persist for more than a month. Each of these things are typical reactions to stress, but for a diagnosis of PTSD, they must be ongoing, have a significant impact on their social or occupational functioning, and not due to medication, substance use, or illness. For a veteran to "have PTSD", at least one, and sometimes several, criteria in each of these areas must be met.

Just because a veteran does not meet these criteria, however, does not mean they are not struggling. This is not a black and white, up or down categorization; the veteran may experience some of these symptoms at one point in their lives, and other symptoms at a different point. That does not mean that "there's nothing wrong" with them. Veterans can and often do struggle with transition out of combat and the military even if they don't meet each of these criteria.

A greater understanding of what PTSD is, and what veterans experience, can provide hope and support to those experiencing it. And that is no small thing.

THE CHALLENGES OF VETERAN MENTAL HEALTH: BEYOND PTSD AND TBI

The mental health and wellness of those who have served in the military is of critical importance to the veteran, their family, and the community in which they live. There has been much discussion in many circles...the media, academia, the professional community...about the impact of combat, traumatic exposure, and military service on the psyche of the military veteran. It is both right and good that this is so; the fact that veterans sacrificed much in service to their country compels us to do all that we can to support them when they leave that service.

That being said, much of the conversation has been focused on two particular conditions: Posttraumatic Stress Disorder (PTSD) and Traumatic Brain Injury (TBI). This is also right and good; both of these conditions, one psychological and one physical, are debilitating, widespread, and insidious. PTSD manifests itself in observable behavioral changes as a result of the automatic response triggered by the limbic system. The veterans, either consciously or unconsciously, say to themselves, "I don't feel safe anymore, so I need to do things that make me feel safe." Hypervigilance, avoidance, seclusion, these are all visible manifestations of the emotional response. TBI, a physical injury to the brain, can lead to cognitive impairment, or the veteran's thought, "I just can't think straight anymore." That old Psych 101 standby, Phineas Gage[1], showed us how physical injury to the brain can impact personality and behavior.

The problem is, PTSD and TBI aren't the whole story when it comes to veteran mental health.

The challenges that veterans face are not just limited to the conditioned fear response generated by PTSD or the cognitive impairment caused by TBI. PTSD does not explain the sense of loss and shame that many veterans feel when they return from combat. TBI doesn't explain the depression that results from a lack of a sense of purpose or alienation from a society that doesn't fully understand what a veteran experienced in the military, let alone in combat. It is critically important to understand the other challenges that veterans face.

We have decades of psychological theory and research to guide us in examining the issues that go beyond PTSD and TBI. This is not an attempt at establishing a Grand Unification Theory of Veteran Mental Health. This is a signpost on the path that may lead to greater understanding of, and therefore better care for, those veterans that we work with.

Later, I will discuss one of the most recent ideas to emerge from observing veteran behavior is the concept of Moral Injury, as described in Jonathan

Shay's book, Achilles in Vietnam[2] and the work of Brett Litz and his colleagues. Moral Injury can be defined as "Perpetrating, failing to prevent, bearing witness to, or learning about acts that transgress deeply held moral beliefs and expectations."[3] In other words, exposure to and participation in combat can cause veterans to change their deeply held core beliefs about what constitutes "right" and "wrong" behavior.

In my experience, another that psychological concept that impacts veterans is the idea of Learned Helplessness, described in many areas but most clearly explained in Dr. Martin Seligman's book, Learned Optimism[4]. The condition is said to occur when someone feels powerless as a result of a traumatic event or repeated failure. Consider learned helplessness in the context of a veteran who is listening to his buddies engaging in a firefight over a radio net, but is unable to do anything about it. Or a Marine who is on perimeter guard, and sees an attack in the distance. Five miles in Afghanistan often could take an hour to navigate, but the veteran feels as though they "should" be able to "get there and do something." After a while, the constantly reinforced idea that any action that the veteran takes will not result in the removal of the aversive stimuli will lead to learned helplessness, and ultimately depression. Then bring the veteran home, when they leave the service, and the thought is, "no matter what I do, I can't get a job" or "nothing I do is good enough for my spouse, so why bother."

Another concept that applies to veterans is needs fulfillment, as described in another one of those old Pysch 101 standbys, Abraham Maslow's Hierarchy of Needs[5]. Rather than focusing on whether or not those needs are met, HOW they are met is a struggle for some veterans. Returning from an environment that is extremely validating, provided the veteran puts forth the effort, a veteran must learn that the manner in which their needs were satisfied in the military and especially during combat is not comparable to the manner in which they need those same needs met in the "civilian world." Physiological needs were often never questioned, as they were often provided to the service member: food, water, these things were readily available, if not always pleasant or palatable. Safety needs? Respond with aggression. Create safety where none exists. Belong/sociological needs were developed within a brotherhood that resulted from close proximity and shared experience…which breaks down quickly upon returning from combat, and is nearly nonexistent when the service member leaves the military. As we climb the pyramid of Maslow's needs, the veteran experiences frustration and anger because the manner in which they formerly met these needs is no longer effective, even though they want them to be effective, because they worked, and the veteran was good at it.

Finally, a huge barrier that I have experienced in a veteran's path towards wellness is an extreme sense of purposelessness. When I first read Frankl's Man's Search for Meaning[6], I was struck by the similarities between his description of concentration camp inmates who had lost the will to live and the sense of purposelessness that veterans experience after leaving the service. When the service member was in the military, they meant something. They were part of something that was bigger than themselves, and they felt personal satisfaction from their service. It was not always fun, and there were certainly some pointless moments, but overall, veterans felt a sense that their lives, their sacrifice, their endurance of hardship were of value and worth. What happens, then, when a Marine who was responsible for the lives of ten of their men and millions of dollars of sensitive equipment returns home, leaves the service, and gets a job washing windows? Or cars? Or construction? Or even something more, a solid job in a bank somewhere or a sales job…but still feels a lack of a sense of purpose? Conditioned response and physical injury to the brain does not describe the sense of frustration, apathy, and hopelessness that comes from a lack of meaning and purpose in a veteran's life.

VETERANS AND MASLOW'S HIERARCHY OF NEEDS

To continue to expand the topic of veteran mental health beyond PTSD and TBI, I will give a deeper look into the mindset of the former military service member by looking at how veterans meet their needs according to Abraham Maslow's Hierarchy of Needs[1]. Maslow's idea is well-known in many other areas: workplace, conflict resolution, learning, and many more. As mentioned previously, it's not my intent to rehash what those needs are, only how they are met.

I realized some time ago that it's not just about what needs we pursue, but how we pursue them.

For those unfamiliar with the military, a large portion of the lower needs on Maslow's hierarchy are provided for the military service member with little effort on their part. If we look at physiological needs, such as food, drink, and shelter, those needs are satisfied nearly immediately. Upon reporting to Basic Training in 1992, after the Army gave me the same set of clothes and haircut as everyone else, they also gave me chow. They gave me a blanket, a bunk, and a locker to put my stuff in. If you were single, you could eat at your unit's dining facility for free, you were given a barracks room. If you were married, the military gave you extra money to pay for the food at the dining facility, you could probably get an apartment or townhome for your family within a week. The military would pay for your hotel in the meantime.

Next up the hierarchy, safety needs: security, order, stability. No question that the veteran had that, or mostly had that. It is extremely difficult to "get fired" (be discharged) from the military service, so there is little danger in abruptly losing your job, unless you violate the rules in some extreme way. Every month, twice a month, you get paid. In the vast majority of cases, the service member knows with confidence when their next paycheck arrives. The military runs on discipline and structure, so the military service member fits right into a routine that has been going since before they got there and will continue well after.

The belonging needs are also a major aspect of a veteran's military service. The bond that is created through shared hardship is well known: Band of Brothers, closer than family. There's something about an old Army buddy that is unexplainable…you can travel across the country and sit on a porch and talk about old times, without skipping a beat. These are mutually supportive and beneficial relationships; they have to be, because during times of stress, those you serve with need to be trusted and relied upon.

Next, esteem needs: self-esteem, achievement, mastery. The military provides many opportunities to stretch you beyond what you think your capabilities are. Obstacle courses. Jumping out of airplanes. Enduring harsh environmental conditions without permanent harm. Learning how to suffer. Each of these things, and more, provides a level of resilience that is supported and strengthened by the encouragement of your friends and buddies around you. During one particular day in the winter of 2008, one of my Soldiers said to me, "Twenty years from now, I'm going to be telling a story about how my bald-headed platoon sergeant made us ruck march through a blizzard." Calling it a blizzard was a bit of an exaggeration. I hold that veteran in esteem. I know that he held me in esteem then and still does now...because my Platoon Leader and I were right there with them. These kinds of events help the service member build mastery and confidence, and give them a sense of achievement.

And finally, self-actualization. There is a level of personal satisfaction that many service members have about their military career, they often engage in personal growth, and have peak experiences that could often approach self-actualization.

Then...they leave the military and now have to learn how to meet those needs in a different way.

Once a veteran has obtained a sense of achievement and mastery in their chosen profession, the military, they then have to pivot to developing mastery in an entirely different arena. A young Marine who led a team in Afghanistan is given the opportunity to lead their own crew for a roofing company, and experiences significant stress because they believe that failure equates to loss of equipment or, even more importantly, loss of life. A Navy Armament Technician who excelled at building explosive ordinance might struggle in an office environment; even though the task is not challenging, it's unfamiliar, and they're not used to not performing tasks well.

Belonging needs? Many veterans feel a sense of alienation from their families and communities. The only ones to "get them" are their buddies and they're no longer around. The bond that is built through shared hardship is not built when no hardship exists. Veterans also learned that, in the military, their peers and superiors were very much a part of their lives 24/7, 365. But when the whistle blows or the clock strikes 5, the veteran's interaction with their civilian supervisor comes to an end. This also leads to a level of disconnectedness and feelings of loneliness.

Continuing back down the hierarchy, to safety needs. Stability is a huge factor for veterans. I'm on my second job since retiring in 2014. I've talked to other professionals, those who had a "successful" transition, in which their first job lasts eighteen months or two years. A colleague of mine, a retired Air Force pilot, has had four different positions with three different agencies, and is about to transition to a fourth, all in the last five years. The stability that the veteran once knew when they were in the military is no longer guaranteed. That loss of stability can be staggering.

Finally, the safety needs. The crisis of veteran homelessness is well-documented. A family of five is no longer provided housing at the government's expense; they are at the mercy of the local housing market regarding availability and price, and depending on where they are, $1,200 a month for a housing budget does not give them the ability to find shelter. Food is no longer provided. The basic physiological needs, which were once unquestioned, are now unsatisfied.

Yes, all humans make choices; we live beyond or means, we choose fast and unhealthy over the deliberate and healthy. We choose the path of least resistance; we cope with stress in unhealthy ways rather than the alternative. The point is often, veterans are unaware of how their former method of meeting Maslow's needs are no longer effective. That leads to frustration. Some veterans feel as if they are starting at ground zero, that their military service was meaningless.

If you are someone supporting a veteran, please take the time to consider how much of a change it can be for a veteran transitioning out of the military or returning from combat. It's not just about getting a job or finding a house; it's about understanding how much of a fundamental shift is required for a veteran to meet the basic human needs that we all desire to have fulfilled.

If you're a veteran what you're going through is 100% normal. It's to be expected. You were once confident, competent, stable, and safe, and you can be all of those things again…you just have to be aware of your own capabilities, and learn new tricks to go along with the old ones.

HELPING VETERANS TRAPPED BY THEIR OWN EXPERIENCES: LEARNED HELPLESSNESS AND VETERAN MENTAL HEALTH

As part of this series that explores the psychological impact of a veteran's military service that goes beyond PTSD and TBI, the concept of Learned Helplessness is a significant factor in veteran mental health. While many veterans are resilient and adaptive, often the constant barrage of negative experiences can wear down even the hardiest of service members.

When I first read Martin Seligman's Learned Optimism[1] these words from that song kept running through my mind. While reading the descriptions of the learned helplessness experiments I asked myself: could the constant stress of combat lead to learned helplessness – stress and burnout?

Through my experience in working with veterans struggling with transition out of combat and out of the military, I feel as though I can answer that question affirmatively.

Serving in the military is highly individualized, but it also provides those who have served with common experiences, both positive and negative. Entering into the beginning of service…Basic Training, Recruit Training, or Boot Camp…each person is de-individualized and provided training to help them become a Soldier, Sailor, Airman, or Marine. Although there are significant amounts of aversive stimuli, such as significant strenuous physical activity, exposure to harsh conditions, restrictive discipline, etc. the recruit soon finds that they are able to avoid this stimuli by performing tasks appropriately and to standard, helping to build resilience and competency.

However, as the veteran proceeds through their military service, there are times when aversive stimuli cannot be removed by any action of the service member themselves. Combat is an extreme example of that, although there are numerous examples throughout the military.

The unavoidable negative conditions can take on as many different forms. I've met veterans who thrived in a deployed environment who struggled in a more controlled and less exciting environment when not in combat. During combat deployments, regular standards, such as pressed uniforms and spit-shined boots, are relaxed. The focus is on accomplishing the mission, whether that's gathering intelligence, assaulting an objective, or providing security escort or overwatch duties. There are rarely formations, organized physical activity, or the structure that comes with military life on the service member's home base. When someone returns from one highly dangerous but less restrictive environment to a less dangerous but more restrictive environment, frustration and helplessness begins to set in. A service member begins to feel "bored" and that the constant repetitiveness of garrison life is "pointless." In order to escape these feelings, many service members turn to maladaptive but seemingly rational coping techniques, such as thrill-seeking behavior or substance use.

Another key element that is commonly experienced by military service members is the concept of "toxic leadership."[2] There are units in the military in which a service member is ruthlessly micromanaged, there is little respect shown, and there is a pervasive sense or meaninglessness and purposelessness. Unlike in the civilian workforce, military service members are unable to resign or quit to get out of an oppressive environment…you're in the unit you are assigned to, and there's little you can do about it. Perfect recipe for learned helplessness.

Combat itself presents an opportunity to experience more helplessness. While deployed to Iraq in 2006-2007, my base, like many at the time, was targeted on a near-daily basis with indirect fire attacks. Rockets and mortars would be fired at our base, a siren would go off, everyone on the base would need to find the closest concrete bunker and wait there until the indirect fire attack was over. Consider the impact on an individual, knowing that at any time a rocket attack could begin, and there was little to do but wait. To hide and wait until the aversive stimuli stops.

Another experience that many service members have while deployed was experiencing loss but being unable to do anything about it. I have talked to veterans who heard attacks on the radio but were unable to do anything about it. I was deployed to Afghanistan in 2010-2011, when a remote base from one of our units was under attack: Combat Outpost Keating, now known as the Battle of Kamdesh[3]. I recall listening to the transmissions of the attack on the radio, and experiencing an overwhelming sense of frustration, and I was hundreds of miles away. There were other Soldiers who were much closer, and felt the frustration to an even greater extent. I've met veterans who saw an attack in the distance, but were unable to prevent it…and still wanted to.

And after leaving the service? The frustration and sense of helplessness continues.

Regardless of whether or not there is a sense of entitlement on the part of a returning veteran, frustration at an inability to get their basic needs met also leads to a sense of helplessness. When a veteran is unable to access basic health care, much less specialty care like mental health services, they can start to feel trapped. When a veteran is unable to find employment, regardless of the reasons, or there are challenges with housing, or they become involved in the justice system due to some of the maladaptive coping techniques described above, they could start to believe that they are, in fact, helpless.

These challenges have less to do with PTSD and TBI, and more to do with the veteran's explanatory style. The good news is there is a solution. As Seligman describes in his book, he found that "helplessness could be learned, and therefore unlearned." Further exploration into how a veteran explains their situation to themselves, whether they are the source of the aversive environment or the source is external, can lead to huge benefits. If a veteran says to themselves, "There's no way I can get a job, because I just can't get along with people anymore," it's unlikely they will attempt to get a job with any level of confidence and enthusiasm. Once the veteran starts to understand the source of these thoughts, and learns they have the ability to challenge them, they can realize they do have more control over their situation than they thought.

If you're a veteran, there is certainly hope beyond the feelings of hopelessness and helplessness that you may feel. If you're a caregiver or mental health counselor, understanding the source of the veteran's sense of futility and helplessness can help you provide the support that the veteran needs. In this way, the veteran, and their family, can achieve the stability and wellness that they both desire and deserve.

MEANING, PURPOSE, AND VETERAN MENTAL HEALTH

Consider what it was like when you first realized that you were part of something bigger than yourself. Maybe it was a team in school, or arriving for your first day at College. It's daunting, it's overwhelming, it's exhilarating. Maybe it's the first time you visit a Civil War or Revolutionary War battlefield, or step inside a church that is centuries old.

That's how many veterans feel about the military.

In my work with veterans, there seems to be a single significant concern: the lack of meaning and purpose in their lives. Veterans are intimately familiar with this, and a recent book, Tribe[1], by Sebastian Junger, articulates this lack of meaning and purpose fairly well.

There is much to be said about meaning and purpose in our lives. While these questions could be just as easily discussed through the frame of reference of philosophy or spirituality, the counseling profession in particular and the mental health professional community in general can certainly support the veteran in determining how to put their doubts about meaning and purpose in place. After all, Jung and Adler were influenced by the philosopher Nietzsche, who was influenced in turn by Schopenhauer. Although William James wrote The Principles of Psychology[2] in 1890, he was primarily considered a philosopher first and psychologist second. Frankl's Logotherapy and the Existential Therapy of Irving Yalom and Rollo May, among many others, can provide mental health counselors the basis for helping veterans when they struggle with these questions of meaning and purpose. It is the convergence of the training and experience of counselors and the understanding of the unique experience of veterans that can provide the understanding that veterans are looking for, a place of purpose and meaning in their lives.

I recall several times in the late '90s, when I was assigned to the 82nd Airborne Division, where I participated in what was called "Division Review." Every unit in the Division was represented on the Parade Field. We assembled by Battalion, and once I was in one of the front ranks: I leaned forward slightly, looked to my left and my right, and realized that I was standing out here in the sun with nearly 15,000 of my closest friends. Not only does that give you a sense of how small you are, it also gives you a sense of how you contribute to one of the most important things you've ever done in your life. I've felt that sense of perspective often; in a sky full of parachutes, crossing the Sava River in 1996[3], touring the Maginot Line[4] in France. Visiting Arlington National Cemetery and Gettysburg. That sense of history, of meaning, of pride that comes from knowing what it is like to be part of something larger than myself.

The simple fact is, veterans miss the military. For whatever reason, no matter how long they've been out of it, there is some part of them that would go back in if they could. Nearly every veteran I've talked to, present company certainly included, have said that they would go back to Iraq, or Afghanistan, or Vietnam, in a heartbeat. Many of them struggle to accept that this part of their life is past, that their war is over. It's as if many veterans are walking backwards in life, looking back on what could be romanticized as their "best" days; they were competent at what they did, they were in the best physical shape they had ever been, and people counted on them.

There is a significant change in someone when they go from doing something that was exciting, challenging, even dangerous at times, to doing something that is less so. When service members leave the military…and it happens to all of them eventually…they do so with a sense of pride and not a small amount of trepidation. They may find themselves in another career, but it may not live up to their own expectations. Without a sense of meaning and purpose in their lives, many veterans can become frustrated, bitter, and angry.

Life in the military is not always pleasant, of course. It's very restrictive, and often both physically and mentally strenuous. There is much sacrifice…separation from family, frequent moves, potentially even the sacrifice of life. Perhaps not every service member who raised their right hand has the same level of dedication to sacrifice, but each of them understands sacrifice in the basic sense. So why would a veteran be nostalgic about a life of nearly constant change, frequent danger, and one that is often unbearably restrictive?

Because, in Man's Search for Meaning, Viktor Frankl quotes Nietzsche[5] when he says, "Those who have a 'why' to live, can bear with almost any 'how'."

Veterans find meaning in the work that they do. In the pride of the unit they're in. In the camaraderie of the brothers and sisters they served with. They understand their purpose, both for small things and for large things. And when they leave the service, they are not certain about how to find that purpose in their post-military lives.

Veterans often find meaning in the places that they've served, and where they and others sacrificed. In 2014, I was watching the televised reports of the fall of Fallujah, and there were three Marines standing there watching it with me; two of them had fought and lost friends in Fallujah. There was certainly anger, but there was also a sense of futility and helplessness…what did we do there? Why did we leave? What, above all, was the worth of the lives that were lost?

Veterans even find meaning in the objects that they've collected while in the service; in their uniforms, coins, plaques and citations. These objects can almost take on a talismanic quality, reminding them of their service while also telling their story without the veteran themselves having to go into too much detail.

PTSD and TBI by themselves don't explain this anger, this helplessness, this frustration, this nostalgia. These questions of "why" and searching for answers are often fundamental to the sense of aimlessness and purposelessness that veterans feel after leaving the service.

When working with veterans, it's important to consider how meaning and purpose in their lives now compare to their sense of meaning and purpose when they were in the military. Understanding each individual veteran's sense of how they explain their service to themselves, and how they explain their current lives, can help that veteran come to an awareness that they no longer have to look back on their service as the best part of their life, but look forward to a stable and purpose-filled future.

MORAL INJURY: THE IMPACT OF COMBAT ON VETERAN'S INDIVIDUAL MORALITY

When a citizen joins the military, whether they are eighteen or thirty, they do so for a number of different reasons. Money for college, desire for adventure, opportunity to leave a negative situation. As with any new endeavor, they bring their "core values" with them. Definitions about what is "right" and "wrong," what is "acceptable" and "unacceptable." Even through the de-individualization process of basic military training, there is a core sense of one's own values that remains relatively unchanged. There are certainly new values that are added, and these are instilled in military service members through repetitive presentation, modeling, and reinforcement. Service members experience a systematic acculturalization that attempts to instill in them "core values" and a "warrior ethos." Even the oaths of enlistment and appointment are action-oriented and value driven.

What happens when these core values are violated in some way? This is the basis of the concept of Moral Injury. If TBI is a physical injury of the brain, and PTSD is an injury that impacts a veteran's behavior, then Moral Injury can most accurately be described as an injury of the soul, an injury of the veteran's core belief. Rather than experiencing cognitive dissonance, the veteran experiences a form of moral dissonance...the actions that they took, or didn't take, are not congruent with how they see themselves or want to believe about themselves.

There are many exceptional books for a further understanding of the concept of moral injury. One is Adaptive Disclosure: A New Treatment for Military Trauma, Loss, and Moral Injury[1] by Brett Litz, Leslie Lebowitz, Matt Gray, and William Nash. It is some concepts from this book that are most beneficial at explaining what moral injury is.

According to Litz et al, there are three primary types of events that lead to the damage about a veteran's core beliefs about what is right and wrong. These three events are: experiencing life-threatening situations, suffering loss in various forms, and committing or witnessing acts that violate that individual's morals and ethics.

Experiencing life-threatening situations is a commonly expected challenge that many service members anticipate upon deploying to combat, and many who have not served in the military understand to be a danger. Some of the challenge in addressing the core issues of a veteran's concerns is this type of event quite possibly be the genesis for that veteran developing PTSD, it is an event that could have caused TBI, AND the veteran's explanation about the causes and response to the event could result in moral injury. One clear example is that when deploying to combat there seems to be a suspension of disbelief that it is actually dangerous. It is not until the first attack, firefight, mortar, or roadside bomb many veterans understand, "this stuff is real." Their sense of safety or "this happens to other people, not to me" that is quickly violated by the reality of the danger of combat. It is this core belief, "I am safe," that is damaged by repeated exposure to life-threatening events, so much so that when the veteran returns to someplace they actually are safe, such as their home or their neighborhood, they tend not to believe it.

The second situation that leads to moral injury is loss in some form. Quite often, it is the loss of a fellow service member…through death, most significantly, but also often through other means. By losing a someone in an abrupt and traumatic way, the service member experiences a significant shock; if that service member is deployed, then that shock is unable to be processed in any meaningful way, because there is no way to escape the environment and no way to avoid continuing to do their duty. The lost buddy is memorialized, their person effects are inventoried, and they will never be forgotten…but they will also never be around. Litz et al describes how veterans become haunted and withdrawn; the replacement service member, if there is one, is not immediately accepted. The "old hands" avoid integrating the new member into the team, in an effort to avoid getting attached. The impact of loss on an individual's core beliefs don't just stop with loss of life, however; the loss of transition is challenging for veterans in many different ways. When a service member is wounded in combat, they are removed from their close-knit group and sent to a medical center. If the wounds are minimal enough, the service member returns fairly quickly, but if severe, then the veteran is removed from the group completely. This loss is significant for both sides…the platoon or unit that the wounded veteran leaves recognizes that there is a "space" there, and the wounded service member feels the pain of separation and worry about how their absence will impact the rest of those they care about. Again, this reaction does not fit the criteria for PTSD, but still is a significant source of shame and withdrawal that impacts veterans.

The third situation identified by Litz and his colleagues is the commission of, or witnessing of, events that transgress a certain aspect of a veteran's closely held beliefs. The extreme egregious acts of atrocities, such as the torture of prisoners and the mutilation or desecration of enemy bodies, certainly fit into this category, but there are other situations that impact veterans. Many veterans travelled in armored vehicles, and in villages, children would approach them to ask for water, food, or candy. And sometimes, inexplicably, pens. Consider a veteran who, after tossing a piece of candy to a little girl, looks back after the vehicles start to move and sees a civilian motorcyclist drive around the vehicles and hit her. The veteran never knew the outcome…whether she lived or died…but automatically assumes the worst, and blames himself for the act. "If I hadn't called her over to give her candy, she wouldn't have been there." There are other challenges, in which veterans feel as though they are helpless to stop horrible things from happening. Between 2006 and 2009, Army Soldiers deployed to Iraq were sent on 15 month combat tours rather than the standard 12, and the later standard 9. Those who were deployed in the earlier part of this time of the conflict were sent to Iraq for 12 months, and then extended for an additional three more. The veterans who lost their friends after the extension were extremely angry…"we were supposed to be home by now"…and blame the Army. Similarly, most routes in Iraq and Afghanistan were given colors to denote their safety, and the least safe of all was called a "black route." Service members who were sent on a black route, and then suffered loss, were extremely angry, and blamed their commanders and higher-level staff for making that call. Similarly, those who did make that call…the commanders and staff…also blame themselves for the loss. These are not atrocities at all, but events that cause these veterans to question their own morals, values, and beliefs.

Blame is a significant aspect of Moral Injury. Someone must be blamed for this life-threatening event, for the loss suffered, for the fact that we could not stop this horrible thing. I'm to blame, he's to blame, they're to blame, it's to blame. Often, veterans believe in this so long they will not be able to assign appropriate blame evenly to all involved, and will most certainly not be able to find any forgiveness. It is with working with a counselor who is familiar of concepts and culture of the military, and addressing these events in a compassionate and safe way, veterans can resolve their moral dissonance and achieve new levels of acceptance and stability in their lives.

THROUGH THE OTHER SIDE OF THE VALLEY OF DEATH: VETERANS AND POSTTRAUMATIC GROWTH

There has been much discussion of the adverse effects on exposure to trauma and combat by veterans. In an all-volunteer force, citizens join the military of their own free will, with varying degrees of understanding about what they may face. Sometimes, the reality of what happens in combat does not match what many service members expect before they get there, and reality tends to set in pretty quickly.

What is less often talked about, but recognized by many service members, is the concept of posttraumatic growth: literally, the experience of significantly traumatic events can and often does generate strength within a veteran. To put it more succinctly, almost verging on cliché, is the old Nietzsche quote: whatever doesn't kill me makes me stronger[1].

There are a significant number of resources available regarding posttraumatic growth; Dr. Martin Seligman wrote about posttraumatic growth in his book, Flourish[2], with some excellent examples from Brigadier General Rhonda Cornum, a Gulf War POW. Drs. Tedeschi and Calhoun[3] have a lot of great information on their website regarding posttraumatic growth, and are leading researchers in the study of the effects of posttraumatic growth.

The key for veterans is understanding how posttraumatic growth has been seen in their own experiences. The things that we witnessed, the things that we experienced, do not need to be crippling, debilitating events that screw our life up; they can be, and often are, significantly life changing events that build our life up. Veterans understand, intuitively, that the traumatic events that they experienced impact them; but a lack of awareness can lead to a downward spiral that can cause the veteran more harm than good.

As humans, in our daily experience, our wellbeing exists somewhere on a continuum between functional and dysfunctional. Many different things cause a shift along that continuum, but for veterans, exposure to major traumatic events without a beneficial response to those events can cause significant decline. Consider the below graphic:

Our veteran starts out at any given point on the spectrum between functional and dysfunctional. How they got there is an accumulation of their life experience. As the veteran progresses in life, trauma occurs; if that trauma affects the veteran negatively, they start to decline. Perhaps the veteran uses unhelpful coping techniques…drinking to forget, engaging in unstable relationships in order to feel connected to someone. Typically, these unhelpful coping techniques lead to another significantly disruptive life event: a DUI, a bar fight, a broken relationship. This causes the veteran to continue to engage in a cycle of unhelpful coping techniques, perhaps leading to more disruptive life events: loss of employment, loss of stable housing. The pattern of disruptive life events followed by unhelpful coping techniques can cause a veteran to end up lower on the spectrum between functional and dysfunctional than when they started.

Consider the alternative, however; if, after the initial traumatic event, the veteran acknowledges the event and acknowledges the changes inside them, becomes aware of the effect that the traumatic event has on their beliefs about the world and their place in it, it is possible that the event can cause them to grow rather than decline. This growth can happen even if a series of events has caused a decline into dysfunction. It would be much better for the veteran, and those around them, for the decline not to occur, but it is never too late to experience posttraumatic growth until it is too late.

If you are a veteran, and are experiencing a series of difficult events in your life after transitioning out of the military, it's understandable. It's common, and even somewhat to be expected. Whatever challenges we face, however, are opportunities for us to improve, to grow, to succeed…if we choose to see them as such. If you are not a veteran, take the time to understand what it means to experience the significantly disruptive events in the lives of those veterans around you, and recognize and support their attempts at posttraumatic growth.

Posttraumatic Stress Disorder is sometimes seen as a debilitating and, all too often, terminal condition. It does not have to be this way; coming out the other side of the valley of death, with all of the scars, tears, pain, and blood associated with it, can be a source of strength. We, veterans, each need to recognize, cultivate, and utilize that strength within ourselves. Individual strength then can be connected with others, and collectively, we can make a real difference in the lives of our brother and sister veterans.

THE STIGMA OF VETERAN MENTAL HEALTH

There has been much discussion over the past fifteen years about the stigma of mental health with veterans and active duty service members. A recent report by the Government Accountability Office[1], which consists of results obtained from 23 focus groups at six locations, indicates that the stigma against mental health is alive and (un)well in the Active Duty Military.

In my experience in working with veterans, stigma exists in two separate areas: the external stigma, which is made up of the collective understanding about veteran mental health in the installation or community, and the internal stigma, the understanding about veteran mental health within individuals. The individual opinion regarding mental health certainly drives the external opinion, and the prevailing impact of the community opinion certainly influences individual opinions.

There are institutional policies that perpetuate the stigma, without intending to do so. Several years ago at my local installation, during the post-deployment processing, those Soldiers identified as needing to see mental health for more in-depth screening were given purple folders, and very quickly everyone knew what these purple folders symbolized. In the GAO report, service members at one installation said that a single elevator accesses the mental health clinic on post, so anyone getting into that elevator is known to everyone else to be seeking mental health. One participant described it as the "elevator of shame." You have to love the bluntness of the military service member, but you know that this description is widely known at that post.

I have had discussions with individuals who have said, "No, we're doing a lot to change that. I mean, Colonels and Sergeants Major openly admit to going to mental health now, it's common." I grant that, there are a lot of higher-ranking individuals going out of their way to make it widely known that they personally don't have a stigma against mental health; but there are a lot of different layers between the Senior Leaders and the troop on the line.

The Soldier Readiness Processing Center on Fort Carson has a long hallway of chairs waiting to see the provider at the end of the day. At Fort Polk, it's a waiting room that's more like a circle, and the line to see the folks at the end of the day snakes back and forth, round and round. I imagine that there are variations on this theme at every military installation in America; after getting your eyes checked, your hearing checked, your blood drawn, and every other conceivable area of health monitored, a service member waits in this line for hours in order to see the provider for ten or fifteen minutes, if that.

When you go into the provider, they ask you the questions: "Having nightmares? Trouble at home? Suicidal thoughts?" Nope, Nope, and Nope. Everything's cool. No issues here…while the entire time, combat is still ringing in their ears, and the voice inside their head is screaming, "just let me get the @#*$ out of here so I can get drunk." Is it every veteran, every time? No, of course not. Many times, things ARE going well. But it is extremely difficult to determine which are truly well, and which are just trying to appear well.

Why is that? Take a look at what happens in that two hour long line while waiting to see the provider for ten minutes. I'm sitting next to my buddy, who I just deployed with for nine to fifteen months. This guy or gal sitting next to me knows me in an intimate way that only someone who has shared combat can know someone. They probably know my favorite MRE, what type of music I listen to, what pisses me off, and what calms me down. They are my brother or sister. I trust them. Or maybe I'm sitting next to my squad leader, who I look up to, and who saved my @#$ a couple of times. They are the closest thing to Audie Murphy that I'll ever know, and I'm pretty sure they could take ol' Audie in a fight any day.

Do you know what that buddy or that Squad Leader is saying? "Better not say nothin'." The ten minutes that we have with a provider we hardly know will never counteract two hours with someone that we trust our lives to. That's the power of the individual stigma; the Department of Defense can say all day that it's okay to seek mental health treatment, but if the idea does not get down to the individual squad and team level, then true change won't happen.

I have a pretty recognizable Jeep Wrangler. Those who know me know what it looks like…and it is likely that, if I were still in the Army, that it would be more acceptable to some of my Soldiers if they saw my Jeep parked in front of a strip club or a bar than it would be to be seen parked in front of the mental health clinic. Is that the way it should be? Absolutely not! But I'm a big fan of reality…and that's the way it is.

So how does that translate now that we're out, or transitioning out? You can take the vet out of the military, but you can't take the military out of the vet. Those core beliefs that we developed while we were in continue with us, become part of who we are. There are thousands of Veteran Service Organizations that will provide case management, help with housing, help with employment, time to take a break from the stress…but how many actually connect the veteran with the mental health services they need? Is the stigma of "crazy combat vet", perpetuated by John Rambo, the Deerhunter, and countless wild-eyed pictures in the news, still alive and well in your community? Is it still alive in you?

The only veteran that I can make sure stays straight is me. I can make sure I take care of myself, change my own opinion regarding veteran mental health, or I can choose perpetuate the stigma. I can join my voice to others who are trying to make a difference, but ultimately, I am responsible for my own voice. You are responsible for yours. The stigma against veteran mental health starts with, and ends with, each of us individually. If you do your part, trust in me that I'm going to do my part.

THE VIOLENCE OF ACTION PARADOX: EMOTIONAL CONTRADICTION OF VETERANS

The violence of action paradox is this: those actions and emotions that protected us in combat are dangerous to us at home, and those actions and emotions that are supportive at home were dangerous in combat.

The military does a great job of training us, but doesn't do a very good job at retraining us after we return from combat. More to the point, we don't do a very good job at retraining OURSELVES after we return from combat or transition out of the service. Without coming to the point of awareness that what we experienced changed us, and that we need to continue to change and grow to succeed, we can become trapped in thoughts and behaviors that were comfortable to us.

If you're a veteran, think about the emotions you had when you were deployed to a combat zone, especially if you went outside the wire. Emotions that were extremely effective there, in combat, but are not helpful here at home. The primary one was anger, of course; it drove us, it fueled us, it kept us awake, and it kept us sharp. Anger is a powerful motivating force that helped us accomplish our mission. Vigilance is another one; being totally aware of what is happening around you, what could potentially happen on the route in front of you, being focused on what happened in this area two hours ago so you can be prepared for something that may happen two minutes from now…it kept us alive. It kept us, and those we were responsible for, safe. It helped us to ensure that the mission is accomplished. As leaders, we modeled aggressiveness and anger as a way to get things done; we may not be very proud of it, if we think about it at all, but we're pretty good at it. We passed along that this is how things got done: The Staff Sergeant on his third deployment taught the Sergeant on his second deployment how to teach the Private on his first deployment to be aggressive. Because it was necessary.

Contrast that to when we come home. How do we turn that anger off if we don't realize that we no longer need it? Stuff makes us angry here. Things happen at home that makes us feel as though we have to be prepared. I can't count how many times veterans I talk to, who have been out of the service for nearly ten years, say, "but I always have to be ready in case something happens." Forget the fact that someone hasn't kicked in my door in a decade, I have to be ready in case it happens in the next few minutes.

What about the other side of the coin? What emotions are acceptable at home, at the park with the kids, walking through the mall, but were dangerous and potentially lethal when we were deployed? A sense of safety is a huge one. Mention the word "complacency" to a combat vet and see what happens. "Complacency Kills" is a phrase you're likely to hear; a mentor of mine in the 82nd used to say, "the moment you stop feeling fear when you think about jumping out of an aircraft is the moment you have to start paying more attention, because you'll start to get sloppy." Feeling safe, feeling like everything is okay and something's not about to happen...that's when stuff really kicks off, and if we were not ready for it when we were over there, then bad stuff happened. Compassion is another one that is absolutely necessary when we come back home, but sometimes got in the way when we were deployed. I'm not saying that all veterans become emotionless sociopathic drones while we were in combat, don't get me wrong. Ill-placed sentiment and compassion towards the wrong people, however, was extremely dangerous, and it was easier to put it off, suppress it, not engage it, rather than deal with the consequences. Realizing that we need to turn these back on, while simultaneously turning off the emotions that protected us in combat, is key to a successful transition.

So the military doesn't do a great job of helping us get to that point of awareness. There are lots of great transition programs, but they are focused on helping us write resumes, dress for success, prepare for an interview. Maybe how to apply to school or submit a business loan. In my experience, however, the military doesn't help us become aware that we no longer need to scan the rooftops; that we don't have to check the security of the perimeter whenever we hear a noise in the middle of the night; that we don't have to use the most effective multi-tool we have, anger, for every situation.

If you're a veteran, and you find that you have struggled or are struggling with this paradox, then reach out to someone. It doesn't have to be a therapist or counselor, although that can certainly help. Reach out to anyone, start talking...but be safe about it. Find someone in your life that you are comfortable enough to tell them anything, while also recognizing that you don't have to tell them everything. If you are a caregiver, or someone who is working to support veterans, the best course of action is to just listen. Don't judge, don't react with shock or surprise, don't respond to their story with, "I know how you feel, because I experienced   ." Just listen. Support. Be present.

Awareness is the key; until veterans, their support network, and their community become aware of the reality of what veterans experience, change cannot happen.

MILITARY VETERANS AND THE DOOMSDAY CLOCK

While at the 2016 Colorado Mental Health Professionals Conference, I had the opportunity to hear Dr. Irvin Yalom speak about his career, psychotherapy, and existentialism[1]. One key point that I picked up on, out of many, is that clients in therapy often do not approach, consider, or talk about, death and mortality.

Not so with veterans.

I am intrigued by the idea of the Doomsday Clock[2]. The Bulletin of the Atomic Scientists puts out periodic updates to this metaphorical "clock", indicating how close civilization is to destroying ourselves through dangerous technologies of our own making. I consider the idea that we, as individuals, have our own conceptual doomsday clock…how much we are aware, at any given time, of how close we are to our own death. While not a perfect correlation with the actual Doomsday Clock, we as humans are sometimes more aware and sometimes less aware of our own mortality.

There are times in our lives when we are acutely aware of how close to "midnight" that we are. These often happen when we are faced with reminders of our mortality, such as near-miss accidents, natural disasters, or serious illnesses from which we recover. Sometimes this happens in the natural course of life, through milestones; the birth of my children, and reflecting on the birth of my children, makes me consider the miracle, and fragility, of life. Attending funeral services, wakes, and memorial services also remind us of the fleeting and transitory nature of life.

Sometimes we are hours away from midnight (I know I was, at age 22 and feeling ten foot tall and bulletproof) and sometimes we are minutes away from midnight when we realize how essentially temporary our lives really are. In his book, The Schopenhauer Cure[3], Dr. Yalom describes a successful, compassionate therapist who is diagnosed with terminal cancer, and spends the last year of his life doing what matters most to him…helping others. At that point, when we inch closer to midnight and are aware of that fact, is when we can truly start to appreciate and participate in life. In Love's Executioner[4], Dr. Yalom writes:

"A real confrontation with death usually causes one to question with real seriousness the goals and conduct of one's life up to then. So also with those who confront death through a fatal illness. How many people have lamented: 'What a pity I had to wait till now, when my body is riddled with cancer, to know how to live!" Irvin Yalom, Love's Executioner

So why this morbid fascination with death? Why not, on a beautiful Colorado day, write about hope, or perhaps transformation? Because the idea rattles around in my head that military service members, regardless of whether or not they served in combat, have a Doomsday Clock set just a little closer to midnight than others. Combat Veterans, certainly, live their lives even closer to that point. Nearly every veteran I meet with has lost someone; until later in my career, I had lost more fellow Soldiers to accidents and illness, and attended more memorial services for non-combat related deaths than I did with combat related deaths. Jumping out of airplanes…now there's an activity that will jump the clock forward a few hours. Military service members, regardless of their reasons for joining the service, quickly become aware of just how dangerous their profession really is.

Of course, after facing combat, the veterans are even more aware of their own mortality. The first indirect fire attack in Iraq occurred less than two hours after we got to the base, and really didn't let up for fifteen months. The sooner that a combat veteran becomes aware of how close they are to midnight, the more comfortable they are to working within those timeframes; and, unfortunately, some veterans even try to push the hands of time even closer.

Maybe they're not aware of it, until someone points it out. Maybe they're not comfortable talking about it, especially with someone whose doomsday clock is set to two hours before midnight. Maybe it is because of the fact that many of their friends have reached midnight, and continue to reach midnight, year after year. We sometimes have the opportunity to see someone else's doomsday clock, and understand exactly how close to midnight they actually are. Viktor Frankl in Man's Search for Meaning[5], describes how he knew that a fellow prisoner had given up on life: in the concentration camp, cigarettes were a form of currency for most prisoners, bartering objects that provide respite, or sustenance. He said,

"The only exceptions to this were those who had lost the will to live and wanted to 'enjoy' their last days. Thus, when we saw a comrade smoking his own cigarettes, we knew he had given up faith in his strength to carry on, and, once lost, the will to live seldom returned."

With everything, though, there is balance. With someone so close to midnight, if they become aware of it, they can choose to actually live. I'm not talking about recklessly sucking the marrow out of life, or cramming an immense amount of pleasure into the draining seconds of life, but to acknowledge that, with the limited time we have on this planet, we can choose to do those things that make us more fulfilled.

If you are a veteran, and disagree, then great! I'd love to hear about it. Many veterans I've talked to, though, recognize this idea. It doesn't make them morbid, it doesn't make them crazy…it makes them human. There's nothing wrong with being a little bit aware of your own mortality, unless you take it too far and midnight comes sooner than it is supposed to by your own recklessness or carelessness.

If you're not a veteran, but work with one or have one in your family, perhaps this is a small amount of insight into their mindset. Maybe this is a chance to become aware of their doomsday clock, to understand in a small way how they think and what they feel. Being aware of our own mortality can be both a blessing and a curse, like many things in this life....and like many things, which it is for us is based on our own internal point of view.

A GENERAL'S MISSION AGAINST MENTAL HEALTH STIGMA CAN'T BE DONE ALONE

An article on the New York Times[1] web site talks about a senior Army leader, Brigadier General Donald Bolduc, how open and forthcoming he is about his experiences regarding mental health concerns, and the treatment he sought to address these concerns. In a recent social media conversation, I talked about how senior leaders, Like BG Bolduc, speaking out about their experiences regarding veteran mental health, is huge when it comes to reducing the stigma against it. Even more to the point, BG Bolduc is the Special Operations Command Africa commander, having spent his career in the Special Forces community. For the leader of a group of the most resilient modern warriors that our military has to offer to speak out and say, "it's okay to seek treatment for mental health" and talk about his own struggles, takes courage and conviction.

In my experience, however, it may not be enough. I never served with BG Bolduc, but his rank, his position, and his experience are enough for me to give him immense amounts of respect. Even more respect for his courage to be open and honest about his struggles. I don't want this in any way to take away from his story or his actions. It's just that I know veterans, both from when I served with them and how I work with them now.

The words, and actions, of a commander are powerful. They set the tone and the culture for the rest of the unit, whether it's a platoon or a regional command. The second most powerful influence: your first line leader.

You see, we can combat the stigma against help-seeking at the command level, by implementing programs, by participating in classes. We can put out all of the PSAs and articles we want, but if that word is not echoed all the way down the chain, then the chain is going to be broken.

When veterans returned from deployment, they are given the Postdeployment Health and Readiness Assessment (PDHRA)[2]. You answer a series of questions, some of them obvious enough to the attentive service member that if they answer it one way, they're in for a long day. If they answer it another way, they get out of there quick. They sit in a long line, waiting to see a provider that they may talk to for ten or fifteen minutes, a provider that they've never met and have no connection to whatsoever. While they're waiting for that provider, though…for an hour or more…they're sitting next to their squad leader. Their buddy. The guy or girl they just deployed with for nine to fifteen months, who knows everything about them. That squad leader was telling them, "better not say nothing" and "see that guy with the purple folder? That means they slipped up and said something they shouldn't have. They're going to mental health." While the Commander is being open and honest, and genuinely encouraging the troops to get the treatment they need, the veteran or service member themselves can think of dozens of reasons why they can't do the same thing.

"Easy for him to say, he's an Officer."

"Bet you he doesn't have to bring back an appointment slip every time he goes to see someone."

"Nobody's going to rag him for being weak, he's the boss."

As I've mentioned before, there are two types of stigma when it comes to veteran mental health…internal and external. The external stigma, the prevalent view of the majority of the military, seems to be changing. The commanders are talking about it, the senior leaders are admitting that they have drinking problems, marriage problems, stress reaction problems, and that they are seeking help to address it. Service-wide Stand Down days, in which units are not training on their mission but instead learning about mental health and wellness, are happening all over the place. Veterans who have taken their own life are now recognized, generally, as casualties in an entirely different kind of war.

The challenge now is with the internal stigma. With the individual veteran, the individual service member who is listening to their buddy say, "there's nothing wrong with you." Or listening to themselves say the same thing. I still hear it: "if I seek mental health treatment, it will hurt my chances at promotion" or "I'll lose my security clearance." If you're a veteran, "If I seek mental health treatment, they'll tell me I can't own guns anymore." Even if that's not the truth, that's what they believe is the truth.

At the end of the article, BG Bolduc relates a story in which he asks a group of Special Forces Operators had been close to explosions while they deployed. All of them raised their hand. He then asked how many of them sought out treatment. None of them raised their hand.

I've had a similar experience. In a meeting with a group of veterans and caregivers, I said, "raise your hand if you know a veteran who has taken their own life." Nearly every single hand in the room went up. As it was a public event, I didn't ask who reached out for help…but I can almost guarantee that it wouldn't be the same amount of hands. There's something fundamentally wrong with that, and there are hundreds of different reasons. It's the current reality of our society, that we are not going to talk about the things we most need to talk about…and not talking about it doesn't mean we stop thinking about it. It often means we think about it more.

I applaud BG Bolduc for his candidness, and appreciate it for what it is. Even he mentions that "there are still the nonbelievers." He knows, because he's been there, when the doors to the team room or the day room or the squad bay shut, the old man is gone, and the Sergeant tells them what's really going on.

When more team leaders, squad leaders and section sergeants say, "it's okay to seek treatment," then we'll really be getting somewhere.

THE PARADOX OF THE VETERAN STORY

Here is the veteran story paradox: Veterans sincerely and adamantly want those that they care about, those they interact with, to know their story and understand their experiences, without having to tell them a thing.

The challenge that veterans have is that they want to be able to tell their story, what happened to them during their military service, while simultaneously feeling that such an effort is totally pointless. Could you imagine that? Experiencing such a significant event in your life that it impacts you almost daily, and both desperately wanting to talk about it while also knowing that no one is going to drag it out of you with a team of wild horses?

Many veterans I've talked to indicate that there are hundreds of reasons why they don't want to talk about the events they had while they were in the service. They want to protect the listener, because if the veteran told the real story, then they would somehow be harming the other person. They want to protect themselves, from the pain of re-experiencing the moment. They want to protect themselves from the listener, from their judgment and condemnation. And of course the listener would judge and condemn the veteran…how could they not? The veteran does that to themselves, after all.

Another reason for not telling the story they desperately want others to hear is the fear that, if telling the story makes the pain go away, then somehow that means the importance of those that they've lost is diminished. "If I don't cry every time I think of them, then that means I don't care about them as much." There are going to be those days. Those anniversaries. Those bad times in the year in which the old veteran lifts their chin, furrows their brow, and allows a single tear to roll silently down their cheek; that never goes away. Those anniversaries have no need to take the veteran to a painful, tormented, get-the-hell-out-of-here-and-leave-me-alone place.

So the veteran is caught between two overwhelming urges: to talk and to not talk. Talking in the past has caused problems; in their relationships, with their family, with their friends. Not talking has also caused problems, in those same relationships, with the same family and friends. The veteran is told, "you're not the same person who went away" and "I hardly know you anymore." The veteran knows this about themselves, and feels exactly the same way.

The veteran also has to pick up and move on. They have to return to their mission, if they're still in the service. They have to get a job, if they're no longer in. The veteran has a need to move on from their experiences, put it behind them, find a career that will give them the same level of fulfillment, meaning, and purpose as their military service did; to ultimately deny that essential part of themselves, their core veteran-ness. To become something that they're not.

Somehow, for the veteran to become a whole new person, this paradox must be resolved. The painful equilibrium of wanting to tell while not wanting to tell has to tip one way or the other in order for them to move on. There are several ways for this to be accomplished.

First, the veteran changes their unwillingness to talk about their experiences. This may happen naturally and willingly; I, for example, am willing to talk about my military experiences, and even the significant emotional events that I experienced, with those that are willing to listen (or read). This takes patience, awareness, and a willingness to answer questions on the part of the veteran. Another way for the veteran to change their grip on the "don't say anything" point of view is to be challenged with an unwelcome consequence if they keep quiet: the loss of a relationship, or yet another relationship. Becoming involved in the criminal justice system…seeking help after thoughts and behaviors get them in trouble rather than before…can also be a motivating factors for veterans to finally address those challenges that they have been experiencing.

Second, the person who wants to listen to the veteran…the mental health professional, spiritual leader, family member…can provide an environment that helps the veteran understand that their worst fears about talking are not going to come true. This is best understood by being completely open to hearing whatever the veteran has to say in an earnest and nonjudgmental manner. For some who are close to the veteran, and who may have had endured hardships of their own, this may not be possible. Spouses of deployed veterans often experienced combat deployments in an emotionally stressful way, so funny stories about video game tournaments and meeting NFL Cheerleaders on Thanksgiving may not be very well received. For those who are not directly emotionally invested with the veteran, however, providing a safe place where the story can be told is critical. Non-judgmentalness is key. If the person listening to the veteran's story cannot keep from reacting with pity or horror at some of the things that they're going to hear, then the veteran will not be able to fully express themselves.

A third way to understand the veteran's experience is to learn about their stories in general through a third observer. There has been unprecedented access to combat veterans throughout the entire span of the wars in Iraq and Afghanistan. Many of those who were embedded with units during deployment have written about their experiences, and told the stories of the men and women they lived with. For anyone who wants to listen to a veteran's stories would do well by coming to an understanding of what it was like for them. Knowledge is the key to understanding someone; a lack of knowledge leads to fear, mistrust, and preconceived notions…even discrimination.

A compromise overcomes a paradox. A willingness on the part of the veteran to speak, a willingness on the part of the listener to hear, and a willingness on the part of both to understand. In this way, the paradox of the veteran's story can be resolved.

VETERANS AND THE RUBBER BULLETS OF OUR THOUGHTS

Have you ever have one of those moments, somewhere between two and four in the morning, when your eyes spring open and you find yourself staring at the ceiling, hoping that you can get back to sleep but knowing that it's probably not going to happen?

Then the thoughts start to come, ricocheting around your mind like rubber bullets. Many veterans I work with experience this exact thing.

Stephen King once wrote a great short story. That's sort of like saying that Ernest Hemingway once wrote a few lines of memorable prose; Stephen King has written MANY great short stories, but the one in particular I've been thinking of is the Ballad of the Flexible Bullet[1]. The basic premise behind the story is that insanity is a type of flexible bullet: insanity is ultimately fatal, but the amount of damage and the length of time that it takes to inflict that damage is different for everyone.

Don't get me wrong; I'm not saying that waking up at three in the morning with a thought you can't get out of your head is insanity or madness. What King's description does make me think of, however, is the damage that thoughts can do to our minds.

I think that many of the thoughts that ricochet around a veteran's mind are like flexible bullets. They're not strong enough to break through the skull, but they're hard enough, fast enough, and large enough to do some damage. The thought starts out small…maybe we hear a song, which makes us think of a buddy, and starts us down a path of memory. It starts out slow as well…we don't intend to get lost in thought for hours on end. And it grows in size, often until we can't recognize its original shape.

I'm certain that this is typical for many, not just veterans. But those who have served in the military…and other first responders, like law enforcement, medical professionals, and firefighters…have more of a likelihood to have experienced events that lend themselves to becoming the core of the rubber bullets of their thoughts.

Once these rubber bullets start to fly, they're hard to stop. They command our attention, which by definition means that we are focusing more on them than other things. And with each pass, with each ricochet that bounces off the inside of our minds, it picks up speed and mass. It distorts into a shape that might be even more destructive, so that the original thought is no longer recognizable. It bounces off our emotions, knocking those over and starting a domino effect. It punches through our self-worth, shredding that, and crashing into self-doubt. It bumps into our memories, triggering more of those, and releasing more rubber bullets to start crashing around our head, the damage increasing exponentially.

One of the ways that I have found to stop the carnage is to let the bullet out.

I work on a lot of projects, both at my office and at home. White Boards are great, and windows will do in a pinch. There have been times when I need to get ideas out of my head and out in the "real world" where I can see them. Yesterday was a perfect example; I have been considering a secondary gain that may come from some plans that we have in motion. I walked across the hall to my program coordinator, just so I could talk it out with her. Did this make sense? Am I seeing it correctly? Where am I going wrong here?

The benefit of getting these thoughts out of our head and into reality, in whatever form…a conversation, a painting, a journal…gives us the ability to evaluate that thought against reality. Without having conscious awareness of the form of the thought, of shape of the thought, we might believe that thought against what we feel to be true.

For example. A veteran feels guilt for taking a certain action while they were in combat. Doesn't matter what it was, because it could have been any number of things, but let's say it's that a buddy got injured because they swapped places on a convoy, or on a patrol. The core of the rubber bullet becomes, "it's my fault that he got hurt. If we wouldn't have changed places, that wouldn't have happened." Let's pause right there, first: what you're saying is, if you hadn't changed places, it would be you that would be hurt. "That would have been better than my buddy getting hurt," is the response of the veteran. So to continue: "it's my fault." Did your buddy ask you to switch, because they were bored of driving? Did the Platoon Leader or Section Sergeant make the swap? Who had responsibility for the change? Often times, not you OR your buddy, but by believing the thought without any evidence, we just keep the kinetic motion of the bullet going. Whose fault is it, when it all boils down to it? The enemy combatant. They bear ultimate responsibility for the actions, not you.

Without having that conversation with someone, you never get to a point where you can look at the rubber bullet. It's like that scene in the Matrix[2] where he stops the bullets and picks one out of the air to examine it. By getting the thoughts out of our heads and into reality, we are able to know just a little bit more about it. Then we can challenge it, if we want to; we may find that our underlying core belief about something is absurd, even without anyone telling us. We may also find that our underlying core belief is true…and then we have to come to terms with that, as well.

If you're a veteran, and you are experiencing the ricochet of the rubber bullet, find someone to talk to. A mental health professional would be great place to start, because they are trained and competent in helping others examine their rubber bullets. Any trusted source, though, someone who can provide a safe place for you to share, is beneficial.

If you support a veteran, be able to provide that space. Give your veteran an opportunity to tell their story, give them an opportunity to take these thoughts out, without judgment or condemnation. Just listening, and being present with them, is both a tremendous gift and an awesome honor.

COMBAT: IT WAS THE BEST OF TIMES, IT WAS THE WORST OF TIMES

For veterans, their time in the service really was both the best and worst of times. Their time in combat, even more so. Dickens[1] had it right; like many fundamental truths that seem to be around, this one resonates.

In a previous post, I talked about what PTSD is: a diagnosable mental health condition that meets certain specific criteria. With a rate of anywhere from 11-20% of veterans meeting this criteria[2], not all veterans have PTSD...but that does not mean that the remaining veterans are not struggling with some form of adjustment or difficulty resulting from their military experience.

Many of the veterans that I talk to understand what I'm saying; they wish those who were not in the military were able to understand this as well. Serving time in the military is very much like immersing yourself into a different culture. The military has it's own expected standards of conduct, it's own spoken and unspoken rules, and even it's own language. It would be as if someone who grew up in Iowa, for example, went to live in England for twenty years, then returned to Iowa. Their personal experiences, their character, would develop by total immersion living in a different culture. It will take some time for that individual to adjust back to a different culture...even more so if they loved living in England.

So veterans struggle with returning to civilian life after the military. Why? What is the problem with just picking up where we left off, using all of the skills that we learned to make a better version of the eighteen-year-old self that joined the military? Because there is something that is fundamentally satisfying about a veteran's time in the service. They meant something. I knew 25-year-old supply sergeants who were responsible for millions of dollars' worth of inventory...who then got out of the service and found it hard to find a job. I knew 28-year-old officers who were responsible for the lives of over 150 soldiers in a combat zone...who then found it tedious to work in a bank. For some veterans, what we were is so much better than what we are...and that's a difficult concept to consider. If we latch onto that idea, like so many veterans do, then we will be forever looking backwards at the best days of our lives, rather than forward to the rest of the days of our life.

Complicate that with the fact that the "best days of our lives" were often pretty bad. Out of my five deployments, my first to Afghanistan was the worst, with my deployment to Iraq making a pretty good case for itself; however, I look back at my time in RC East with fondness, pride, grief, and, yes, pain. I tell funny stories about the time a pack of donkeys was weaving in and out of our security patrol, calls of "Donkey passing on the left" going out over the platoon net. I tell stories of skill, bravery, honor, and courage. When the discussions about women in combat start, I talk about my driver, one of the bravest women I know, dismounting the vehicle behind me just to watch my back. I tell stories of monkeys, MREs, stupid movies that were watched over and over again, and remember the beauty of the country.

Veterans talk less often about the other stuff, the hard stuff...but think about it more often. The bad comes just as often as the good, if not more so. A veteran does not have to have PTSD to experience grief at the loss of a buddy, or frustration at the fact that they find it difficult to readjust to society. When veterans leave the service, many of them feel as though they have lost their sense of purpose. They were once counted on, depended on, they were good at what they did and they loved it. They were important...and losing that sense of accomplishment, that sense of importance, is very difficult.

Think about the inspirational speeches that you have heard throughout the years: the Saint Crispin's Day speech from Henry V[3], Patton's speech to the Third Army[4] or Theodore Roosevelt's Man in the Arena speech[5]. If you're a veteran, and you're like me, something stirs inside of you at the thoughts and ideas presented there. The sound of Taps, while painful, is also beautiful. The sound of Amazing Grace, played on bagpipes, is simultaneously one of the greatest and worst songs in the world.

Just because a veteran does not have PTSD does not mean that they are not struggling...taking the time to understand that struggle, and to hear a funny (or not so funny) story, can lift the burden just a little bit.

THE GUNS DO NOT GO SILENT AFTER COMBAT…NEITHER SHOULD VETERANS

Everyone has a story. You just have to listen to it.

As a mental health counselor working exclusively with veterans, it often surprises me how difficult it is…and also how easy…for a veteran to be able to tell their story.

The impacts of combat, deployments, or even just military experience in general are felt long after a veteran leaves the service. When I say that the guns do not go silent after combat, I don't mean that every veteran experiences John Rambo-like flashbacks every time a bottle rocket fires off, even though that's a thing. I mean that our experiences in the military are hard-wired in our brain, and they crop up at really strange times. There is a certain type of weather pattern, an early-morning-post-rain kind of thing that reminds me of Airborne School at Fort Benning, Georgia in February of 1997…if that's not a specific memory trigger, I don't know what is. And it's not just a memory…it's an embodied experience, in which my body feels the memory, rather than just pictures in my head.

There are thousands of things, big and small, that can take a veteran back to their time in the service, some good, and some admittedly bad. The problem is, if we are not aware of them, then getting lost in these memories can drag us down rather than empowering us to do more. Veterans can and should acknowledge these memories as valued life experience, rather than shackles that bind them to the past.

"Easy for you to say," I hear you mutter. I know. I get it. The memories of loss, or pain, the memories of things that we saw or things that we did are difficult to overcome. It is a challenge to see those moments as beneficial, but see them that way we must, or else they can bury us with their weight.

That's where the talking comes in. Have you ever sat on a porch and talked to an old Army buddy? The benefits of recounting a shared experience are significant. It amazes my wife that I can not talk to someone for a couple of years, and we can get on the phone and pick up a conversation as if we never left off. The challenge there, though, is that it becomes an echo chamber, with the stories only being told to those who were there.

In his book, Tribe[1], Sebastian Junger talks about an idea that I think is pretty intriguing. The opportunity to let veterans speak.

…[what may be] "More dignified might be to offer veterans all over the country the use of their town hall every Veterans Day to speak freely about their experience at war. Some will say that war was the best thing that ever happened to them. Others will be so angry that what they say will barely make sense. Still others will be crying so hard that they won't be able to speak at all."

Could you imagine the power behind each individual story, and the collective impact of the entire event? It would be helpful for both the veteran and the community to be able to hear this. And, in my opinion, it shouldn't just be left to those veterans who served in combat. There are thousands of veterans who joined the service, did their four years or six years or whatever, and got out and continued on with their lives.

Being able to tell your story means that you feel safe enough to tell your story. That you won't be judged, or ridiculed, or pitied. As I've mentioned elsewhere, veterans are not some fragile eggshell that must be handled with delicacy. We are strong. Resilient. For many of us, quite literally battle-tested. Who wouldn't be changed after seeing what veterans have seen or experienced what they experienced? That doesn't make us weak, though. It doesn't make us fragile…it makes us real. To be able to tell our story, though, we need to be able to know that when we start talking about stuff, the real stuff, that the other person is not going to recoil in horror. The only thing that does is reinforce in the veteran's mind that what is in our thoughts is horrible, and that we shouldn't say it.

Others of you might say, "well, veterans should just get over it. They knew what they were getting into." I've heard it before. Everyone has a right to their own opinion, and I'm the last guy to condemn them for it. The problem is, I know that I didn't know what I was getting into, even though I thought I had a pretty good idea. There is a huge gap between theoretical understanding and lived experience, and no amount of reading, watching, or training can prepare someone for the complete, total-body, full sensory experience of military service. I was talking to a veteran recently, and they said it clearly: "they don't get it, because they haven't lived it."

And we don't want them to. That is one of the paradoxes of being a current era veteran: we want people to know what it was like for us, while simultaneously not wishing our experiences on our worst enemy. The way to do that is for veterans not to stay silent.

If you're a veteran, figure out a way to let your voice be heard. Write it out, like I do here. Paint it, on a canvas or on a wall. Sing it, shout it, turn it into an interpretive dance if that's what you want to do. Just tell your story, somehow, in some way.

Just because the echoes of the guns are still ringing in your ears, doesn't mean that you can't drown them out by the power of your voice.

THE VETERAN DIVIDE

There seems to be a gulf, a divide, between veterans and those around them. I think the reasons for this divide are numerous, and many are unnecessary.

In many cases, a veteran creates this divide themselves, by isolation. Seclusion. Withdrawing. By assuming that there is no way that anyone other than those with shared experience would be able to understand. Veterans can create this divide by demanding that their needs be met, a sense of entitlement. Maybe not a sense of entitlement, but a sense that their sacrifice and their choices should mean something to those around them. The more resistance there is in getting these needs met, the more strident the demands to have those needs met; the more strident the more resistant, until there is a hardening of positions on either side.

The community, the "other" is also causing the divide. "Veterans should not act this way," I've heard people say. "They volunteered for what they did, they made their bed, so now they must lie in it. After all, I made my choices". Individuals without a frame of reference or understanding of service members must require the veteran to change: "there is no reason for them to be the way they are, don't they know it's safe here?" Just because you say that it's safe doesn't mean that veterans know that, or even that it is safe. You may be lacking knowledge of the dangers around; maybe it is you that are oblivious, rather than the veteran.

So here are the two sides, locked into a never-ending tug of war. A stalemate. The veteran and the non-veteran, neither side understanding the other or even willing to try. What to be done?

This is the imperative. The requirement. Should. Must. Someone should give me a job, after the hell I went through. I've proven myself as a leader in the military; therefore I should be a leader in my next career. On the other side, veterans should just get over the war. They must learn to be okay with how we do things; they must conform to our way of thinking. Even without conscious awareness, we think that these musts and should are imperative and incontrovertible.

So how to change it? Let's look at an example from the view of psychology. Irvin Yalom, in The Gift of Therapy[1], states, "Therapy is enhanced if the therapist enters accurately into the patient's world." Is the corollary true…that therapy is diminished if the counselor does NOT enter accurately into the patient's world, or enters the patient's world inaccurately? The therapist is on one side of the gap, and the veteran client is on the other side of the gap. If the counselor does not cross over that gap, by whatever means possible, and hang out on the veteran's side, then it is challenging to eventually help the veteran to move over to the mental health professional's side. The side of wellness and stability. If I reach out and attempt to drag a veteran over to my side, where I know things are great, and where they would be much better off if they would just get over here, then the veteran is going to resist. What's so great about my side? I haven't even taken the time to figure out what makes it so good on my side.

Alternatively, if I as a counselor, or someone who is interested in bridging the gap, moves over to the veterans side, understands their point of view, comes to an understanding of how the veteran sees the world, then there will be the opportunity to explain the benefits of your point of view. There is the possibility to integrate both sides into a new way of thinking or method of operating.

How can someone accurately enter into a veteran's world by making assumptions about that veteran's experiences, and acting upon those assumptions as if they were the truth? Perception breeds reality. Here is an example that I often use: There are times, when I'm lost in thought or focused on a particular situation, that I can come off as brusque, stand-offish, or unapproachable. It's nothing personal, just my nature when I'm in my thinking space. Others can interpret that as being rude, or being a jerk. And what happens when you see someone acting like a jerk? You treat them like a jerk. I'm really not…I'm a pretty good guy when you get to know me…but no one likes being treated like a jerk. You know what happens when I think I'm being treated like a jerk? I act like a jerk.

How can anyone truly partner with someone if they make judgments based on a preconceived notion of how that particular group of individuals is "supposed to be?" If all veterans have PTSD, or all men of color who grew up in an urban environment are criminals, how much do you think that causes the individual being judged to solidify their position? After all, the person doing the judgment is confirming a preconceived notion about prejudice and close-mindedness in the eye of the one being judged. Trust is eroded, not built.

If you see me as a hero, I'm going to deny it. If you see me as a victim, I'm going to reject it. If you see me as a villain, I'm going to refute it. Each of these three stereotypes that veterans are often categorized as creates an automatic defensive reaction. It shouldn't be that way, you say? Who says? You, because it's your position? You have a right to your opinion, absolutely, but you also have a responsibility to accept the consequences of that opinion. Maybe you're not aware of the consequences, and that's fine, but that doesn't mean the consequences don't exist.

Any category that marginalizes someone without greater understanding of the situation behind the individual being in that category is rigid and judgmental. If there is a gulf, a divide, between veterans and their community, then the best possible way to overcome that gap is for everyone to be bold enough to step into that gap. To compromise, to change, to come to a greater understanding about the other's position.

Without attempts on both part to bridge the gap, the gulf will continue to widen, to no one's benefit.

FOR VETERANS, SUCCESS OR STRUGGLE IN TRANSITION CAN DEPEND ON MENTAL HEALTH

Previously, I've talked about how awareness is the key to recovery for veterans, I've joined with others talking about what PTSD is and what it isn't, and I've attempted to describe what happens emotionally to veterans when they return from combat. All of these are an attempt to support veterans in transition out of the service to understand: you are not alone. There are hundreds of thousands of veterans transitioning out of combat and out of the military, and many of them are experiencing similar challenges.

This is also an attempt for those who are not veterans…family members, for example, or those who have never served but support military service members and veterans in any way they can…to understand a little bit more about what veterans experience, what they think and feel. Many veterans struggle with how to explain how their experiences changed them…as much as they want people around them to understand, they also don't want to, and don't know how to.

Veterans sacrificed. It's what they did, and what they want to continue to do, to serve. Being served, especially regarding mental health, takes determination on the part of the veteran, and understanding on the part of the mental health professional.

The bottom line is this: stability in a veteran's mental health is a key factor in the success, or failure, of their transition. There are literally hundreds of nonprofits addressing what can be described as the "wellness" needs of veterans: resiliency camps, days out at the ballpark, fishing trips. There are excellent nonprofits that help veterans give back to their community, such as Team Rubicon and The Mission Continues, which is a great opportunity to connect with other veterans and regain that sense of community that many of us miss after we leave the service. How many organizations, however, help connect a veteran with a mental health professional so they can truly explore how their experiences have affected them?

Two outstanding programs, Give an Hour[1] and The Soldiers Project[2], support veterans by connecting them with mental health professionals who provide free services to veterans. These organizations rely on the support of the mental health professional community, however; it is incumbent upon the provider community to bear the cost of providing treatment. The VA Vet Centers[3] are outstanding resources, but are limited in the type and number of veterans they can serve. There was recently an announcement about the Cohen Veterans Network[4] that is going to set up clinics around the U.S. to support veterans; an excellent opportunity for veterans to get the support they need.

You see, we can house veterans, we can join together with the excellent work that LinkedIn is doing and connect veterans to employment, we can support the veteran's needs when they become involved in the legal system…but what about the underlying causes for veteran homelessness, unemployment, and justice involvement? That is where the mental health professional community can support.

I hear what you're saying, because I hear veterans say it all the time: "I don't need no shrink. Therapy is a bunch of psychobabble crap. There's nothing wrong with me that a stiff drink and isolation can't take care of." Meanwhile, we're flying off the handle when we trip over one of the kid's toys, shop at midnight to avoid crowds, and follow a prescribed path from work to home day in and day out. That's not living…that's existing. So why would we avoid taking advantage of something that will help us live, help us recover, help us understand how combat and our service changed us?

"Well, therapists don't get me. They don't understand what I went through, and I don't feel like trying to explain it." My response: how do you know if you don't check it out? I have experienced some colleagues who want to help veterans, but don't understand military culture, sure…but the vast majority of my colleagues that I have spoken to DO understand. They have taken the time to learn at least the basics of the military mindset; and on top of that, they are trained and experienced professionals who want to support veterans in their search for wellness and recovery. But if you have needs in other areas of your life, you keep looking for someone you like to help you until you find the right person. When my wife and I were buying our house, we started working with one realtor that we didn't particularly click with…but we needed a house, so we kept looking until we found a realtor we liked. You look for a good mechanic, and don't stop until you find one, because the car needs to be fixed. Why do veterans then stop at one therapist? The house still needs to be bought, the car still needs to be fixed, you still need to find a place of stability in your thoughts and emotions.

Veterans are not broken-winged birds, we are not a three legged dogs, we do not need coddling or protection from the big, evil world. It's not necessary, and it's certainly not wanted. Veterans have seen, and many continue to think about, some of the most horrendous acts that one human being can do to another. You don't go through something like that and come out the other side unchanged…but that doesn't mean we're damaged, or somehow broken or flawed. It means that we have had a natural reaction to real life; and seeking help for how that changed us is not something that turns us into that broken-winged bird, either.

I support and applaud all of the veterans who are attempting to make the transition from the military to your new civilian careers. You are being the proactive, problem-solving professionals the military taught us to be. But for every veteran who successfully transitions, I can all but guarantee that you know a former battle buddy, flight crew member, ship mate, who struggles with addiction, homelessness, or suicide.

By all means, go to the ball park, enjoy a fly fishing trip, ride horses and pet dogs...but know that none of those things, by themselves, will help you recover from what you have experienced. Allow a mental health professional to help you come in from the fight for a few minutes, set down your pack, take off the body armor, and take a knee. Perhaps your life depends on it.

FOR VETERANS, OUR CAPACITY FOR STRESS IS GREATER THAN WE KNOW

The human capacity for stress is much greater than what we individually believe.

Was there a time where you thought that you weren't going to be able to accomplish something? You were at your limits, emotionally, physically, mentally, spiritually?

You're still here, aren't you?

Life is challenging, and it's even more challenging when we choose to put ourselves in stressful situations. This is what amazes me about veterans is that we find ourselves in some of the most extreme, tense, and stressful moments in life, and sometimes don't even realize that it was our choices that placed us in that moment.

Think back to basic training or boot camp. It might have been intense, or not so much, but it was certainly…instructive. It could have been possibly the most challenging thing that you experienced in your life up to that point. With the exception of older veterans who were caught up in the draft, the majority of veterans today made that choice.

Just when you get through that, though, and you feel like you're prepared for anything, the military continues to throw more curve balls at you. Permanent Change of Station[1]. Foreign countries. Responsibility. Relationships. The need to balance personal life and professional life when the two are so impactfully intertwined. I recall my first duty station in Germany, I was walking through downtown Mannheim one day trying to read the signs and getting thoroughly confused. I knew what the letters were, but I had no clue what they meant! It's a really strange feeling to be betrayed by the alphabet you've known your whole life…but we manage those stressors. And it makes us stronger, more resilient, more capable. More professional.

Our individual capacity for stress is like a bathtub. Everyone has a limit to how much stress they can contain, and it's different for each person. For some, the size of the bathtub is like a teacup. For others, the size of the bathtub is like the room you're sitting in. No matter the size of your bathtub, it is going to be filled by life's stress. There are two ways to get water out of a bathtub, though…the "wrong" way, by filling the tub up so much that the water spills over the top and makes a huge mess, and the "right" way, of unblocking the drain and letting the water go where it wants to.

Oh, and did I mention that the bathtub is made of rubber? That the size is flexible? My capacity to handle stress was much less when I was 18 and going through Basic Training, compared to when I was 33 and going to Iraq for the first time. I had a long time between those two events to expand my capacity for stress, to increase the size of my bathtub.

The key to managing the stress of life is first recognizing that we are reaching our limit, and the second is figuring out how to reduce that stress in a constructive way. Many times, we are not aware that our stress is about to overflow the tub until there is a huge mess in the bathroom, and we have to deal with it. We're not always the cause of it directly…we can blame life, we can blame others, we can shake our fist at the heavens but we still have a mess to clean up. Figuring out a solution to keeping the tub from overflowing is much easier, in the long run, than raging and blaming.

Have you ever dropped a solid object in a container of liquid? If the tub is full, and you drop a block of concrete in it, then it's going to overflow. We may be able to handle one block, perhaps two blocks, but then things seem to start getting overwhelming.

So you have your tub. The faucet of life is constantly running, stuck in the open position, filling your tub with the stress of the daily grind. Bills to be paid, kids to get to school, work to be done. Then, drop an unexpected problem into the tub; you get a ticket. You're about to get out of the military, which you've never done before; you're about to have another kid, the cost of living is too high where you're currently stationed, and the future is uncertain.

Recipe for disaster, right?

The thing about realizing our capacity to handle stress is that, in the exact moment we need to remember that capacity the most, we recognize it the least. We are so focused on the current challenges that we don't take a break, step back, and look at everything in it's proper perspective. That moment of pause to recognize, let's look at everything I've been through…how does this compare to that? You say to yourself, "I had seven different jobs in five years while I was in the military. I am experienced at picking up and moving to a new town, getting started in a new place. I have handled bigger things than this."

After so many experiences of "I can" and "I did", why is it that we still have "can't" in our heads? The anxiety, the nervousness of the uncertain future freezes us as if we getting off the bus (or cattle car) at Basic Training all over again. We made it through then…what is keeping us from getting through it now?

Sometimes it's the should. I should be able to handle this on my own. I should be strong enough, smart enough, good enough to take care of this. I should not need help. I don't need to go to the doctor for this pain in my foot, I don't need to go to a therapist for these thoughts in my head. Sign of weakness, have too much to do, what others will think.

What happens when the tub overflows?

FOR VETERANS, REMEMBERING OUR UNWAVERING RESOLVE CAN DRIVE OUR SUCCESS

Above all, we must realize that no arsenal, or no weapon in the arsenals of the world, is so formidable as the will and moral courage of free men and women. -Ronald Regan

Veterans love our Creeds. The Marines have their Rifleman's Creed[1], The Army has the Creed of the Noncommissioned Officer and the Soldier's Creed[2]. Each of the other services...Air Force, Navy, Coast Guard...have their own Creeds. There are several similarities, and quite a few differences, but one of the key connecting factors is something that I never quite understood before: an iron resolve to be, to do, to accomplish. The imperative WILL.

As an Army veteran, I am most familiar with The NCO Creed and The Soldier's Creed. Of the many important and critical lines in the NCO Creed, one of the most important to me was always: All Soldiers are entitled to outstanding leadership: I will provide that leadership. The central part of the Soldier's Creed makes up the Warrior Ethos of the Army: I will always place the mission first. I will never accept defeat. I will never quit. I will never leave a fallen comrade. The key word in each of these lines: WILL.

The NCO Creed does not say, "I may provide outstanding leadership" or "I choose to provide outstanding leadership at some points, but not at others." The Warrior Ethos does not say, "I might sometimes place the mission first" or "I may quit". The word, and concept, of WILL, indicating an iron and unwavering resolve, is repeated throughout each of the service's individual Creeds.

Starting with the Oath of Enlistment that each enlisted member of the Armed Forces takes, regardless of service: I WILL support and defend the Constitution of the United States against all enemies, foreign and domestic; that I WILL bear true faith and allegiance to the same; and that I WILL obey. The Oath of Office that all Commissioned Officers are required to recite upon commissioning has this imperative as well, stating that they "WILL well and faithfully discharge the duties of the office upon which" they enter. There is no question and no grey area about what is going to happen.

Throughout the Creed of a United States Marine, the imperative of the word WILL is repeated several times, including "I will..." at the end of the third line, "We will hit..." and repeatedly throughout the entire Creed. The unquestioning WILL is indicated with the phrase, "I will ever guard it against the ravages of weather and damage as I will ever guard my legs, my arms, my eyes, and my heart against damage." There is no "may" here, no "might" or "could possibly"...only the certainty of will.

Short and to the point, the Sailor's Creed[3] indicates the imperative by repeating the Oath of Enlistment and Oath of Office in the dedication of supporting and defending the Constitution and the United States of America, and obeying the orders of those appointed over them. The long and storied history of the Navy is also represented in each Sailor's awareness, stating, "I represent the fighting spirit of the navy and those who have gone before me to defend freedom and democracy around the world."

Sometimes the imperative is represented by what will not be allowed, rather than what will be done. The Airman's Creed[4] repeats, "I AM" several times and concludes their creed with: "I will never leave an Airman behind, I will never falter, and I will not fail." There is no question the resolve behind these statements.

The Creed of the United States Coast Guardsman[5] also repeats the imperative WILL several times, and even uses the imperative SHALL. In a phrase that speaks to this old Sergeant's heart, the Coast Guardsman states, "I shall sell life dearly to an enemy of my country, but give it freely to rescue those in peril." The Coast Guardsman does not say that they "may, perhaps, sell life dearly." They say that they are going to. Without a doubt.

There is something admirable in this uncompromising will represented in each of these Creeds. This is the drive of sacrifice. This is the drive of service. This is the drive that is within each and every service member, and sometimes is unfathomable to those who have never served in the military. The WILL in each of these Creeds is represented in the look of determination in each service member's eyes as they gather their determination to accomplish a task, and is represented in each tear shed at the playing of Taps. The iron resolve of WILL is represented in the salute of the World War II and Korean War veteran on Memorial Day, each weathered hand and straightened back knowing exactly what the cost of exercising this will entails, and it is represented in the upraised hand of the newest recruit and commissioned officer, who have yet to fully understand the meaning of the imperative that they are reciting.

Do all service members live by these words? Sadly, no. If that were the case, there would be no inter-service crime, there would be no sexual harassment or Military Sexual Trauma. There would be no toxic leadership. Of the many things that I am, a realist is certainly one of them, and I am not of the camp that thinks that service and sacrifice can cover a multitude of sins.

What I do believe in is the basic honor and integrity of those who have served in the military, and choose to assume honor in them until proven otherwise. For those who did their duty, praise and respect are rightly deserved.

Getting out of the military though…did we lose that will? Did we lose that iron resolve, the desire to action, that indomitable capability that we found in our various boot camps and basic trainings, and in innumerable experiences throughout our service? Did we lose the values that were instilled within us, not through repetition of mindless phrases, but by recognition of the stirring of our soul? Whether you served three years or thirty-three, the values you learned in the service can serve you well in life. The imperative, the "I AM" and "I WILL," make you a strong individual, capable of overcoming great adversity and achieving amazing things.

The only thing that you need say to yourself: "I Will Remember."

TWO TYPES OF LEADERSHIP, AND HOW THEY APPLY TO VETERAN MENTAL HEALTH

If there is one thing that veterans know, it's leadership. Good leadership, bad leadership, toxic leadership, inspirational leadership. The concept of leadership is hardwired into the military's hierarchical system, and is one of the core elements of success of America's modern military. In my experience, those who haven't served in the military have a misconception that military leadership is all about blind obedience, that veterans are all mindless zombies that follow orders without question. Nothing could be further from the truth; in my 22 year career, I've had great leaders, mediocre leaders, and some pretty terrible leaders. This is because, like every other organization on the planet, it's made up of humans, and humans aren't perfect.

Leadership theory, leadership styles, the theoretical aspects of leadership, all of these are huge when it comes to motivating others. Acknowledged leadership experts like John C. Maxwell[1] and Simon Sinek[2] have established well-deserved reputations for helping others understand the concept of "leadership" and how to apply it to their lives. Hanging out in the shadows of giants, as I am, there are only two very basic types of leadership that I want to talk about today: transactional leadership and transformational leadership.

Transactional leadership, in the military, was pretty common. Do what I say, and you get stuff you want. Don't do what I say, and you get stuff you don't want. It was a very straight, give-and-take kind of relationship. I was pretty surprised early in my career in the Army: "you mean, all I have to do is show up on time, do what I'm told, and I get promoted? I can do that!" Transactional leadership is based on actions that will either bring rewards or punishment. By doing what I'm told in the Army, I was rewarded: promotions, time off, recognition, respect. I was once even given tickets to a Rolling Stones concert in Germany for winning a Soldier of the Quarter board. By contrast, if I don't do what I'm told, the reverse happens…promotions become demotions, time off is taken away. The challenge with transactional leadership is that it only lasts as long as the rewards have value and the punishment is aversive in the eyes of the individual being led. Transactional leadership can quickly bring out initial compliance, but is not sustainable. How many times have you seen a bunch of Soldiers or Marines working like ants when the Gunny or Platoon Sergeant is around, but then slack off as soon as they're out of sight?

Transformational leadership, on the other hand, was not found to be as common in the military. Those leaders who inspired us to work beyond our limits, not because we had to (transactional), but because we wanted to.

Transformational leadership occurs when the change is much more internal, the thoughts and values of an individual are changed, rather than just be behavior. Transformational leadership is harder to develop, and less straightforward to apply, but it last much, much longer than transactional leadership. Not just a throwaway "winning of hearts and minds" approach, but a very real environment of mutual respect and honor. We all know some leaders who we were willing to walk through hell for, and those are the ones that we still remember long after we leave the service.

There is nothing that says any one leader can't be both. There were some Soldiers that I led who only responded to transactional leadership, and were not influenced by transformational leadership at all. There were some service members, like me, where transactional leadership didn't gain much traction, but transformational leadership could keep me going for days. Each leader is different, each follower is different, and there are even times when a leader must be flexible enough to apply the different styles of leadership with the same individual at different times. Starting with transactional leadership and slowly transitioning to transformational leadership is the key to sustained desired change.

So what does this have to do with veteran mental health? "You're a mental health counselor, not a leadership coach," I hear you say, and you're right. The strange thing is, in my experience, veterans seeking mental health with a professional react in many of the same ways.

When a veteran first comes to my office, it's many times because things aren't working well. "I'm only here because I have to be," they say, many times because they want to save their marriage, or are struggling at work, or got in trouble with the law. They come in because they have to, not because they want to...transactional. Just like in leadership, this is a behavioral change without much corresponding change to thought or internal values. At some point during our work together, however, the shift between transactional compliance and transformational compliance happens. Some sooner, some later, but when the veteran gets to the point of actually wanting to change how they view the world, how they think and feel, then the magic starts to happen. When the veteran realizes, "I'm doing this for myself, not for anyone else" and "I'm doing this because I want to, not because I have to," that's when real change can happen in their lives.

If you're a veteran, and things don't seem to be going quite right in your post-military lives, is it because you're stuck in an old way of thinking? Is it because you've learned to be rigid and inflexible? Talk it over with someone. Getting to the point of change because you want to, and not because you have to, will be much more fulfilling and long-lasting, and much more pleasant than the challenges you're currently facing.

PERCEIVED VERSUS ACTUAL CAPACITY FOR ENDURING HARDSHIP

The thing that amazes me about veterans is their ability to put up with some of the most challenging situations any individual can face. You can put them in any environmental condition, expose them to extreme levels of psychological stress, and yet they'll still keep moving forward.

To many veterans, this is both strength and liability.

I've often thought about how to describe military culture to those who have never served, and it is challenging. There is a saying veterans have: to those who have been there, no explanation is needed; to those that have not, no explanation is possible. After the end of the draft, fewer Americans have served, or have had direct family members who have served in the military. With each successive generation, our nation's direct experience of veterans is diminishing.

The citizen enlists in the military. The reasons for this are many; to get out of a dead-end town, to serve your country, because your family served, to pay for college, to see excitement, adventure, really wild things. For some, it is as much of a running from something as a running to something, a way to break the chains of the environment they find themselves in. Once they get to basic training, though, the reasons and motivations that brought them there become secondary to the task of transforming a civilian into a military service member. We can debate about the horrors of war or the necessity of a standing military, but the truth is that there has always been a need for warriors in any society, and there always will be. Basic Training, Boot Camp, is the transformative process that creates those warriors.

Not everyone makes it through initial military training. When I went through Basic Training in the early '90s, there were plenty of ways to get out of the military. Some were behavioral…break enough rules, and you were out…and some were psychological. While the desire to quit was often present, the actual act of quitting happened rarely, and it was of course not celebrated. Sometimes stuff happened, like an injury, which caused someone to be discharged against their will. Each of these come together in complex and challenging ways, to the ultimate result: those who completed basic military training were those whose internal or external environment would not allow them or did not require them to quit.

After a service member's basic training, they are sent to advanced training. Basic training gives military service members exactly that: basic military skills such as weapons familiarity and marksmanship, physical conditioning, discipline, marching, etc. In addition to all of those things, however, each service member has an occupational specialty in the military: driving trucks, collecting intelligence, engaging in combat, hundreds of other advanced specialties. Again, this is a selective process; while a service member may have passed through basic training, they may not be able or willing to meet the requirements of the advanced training and are then sent to do something else; but quitting happens relatively rarely.

This process of enduring hardship continues through a veteran's time in the service, whether it is five years, fifteen years, or twenty-five years plus. Each of us has our own individual capacity for enduring hardship, and it's often much greater that we actually realize; military service stretches individuals by putting them in situations that provide hardship beyond their known capacity but within their actual capacity. Throughout any one particular veteran's career, there are thousands of choices to do or not do, pursue or not pursue an opportunity.

As I mentioned before, however, it is this capacity for hardship that is both a strength and a liability. If a veteran who has experienced the admittedly minor hardship of basic military training, they may feel as though they can accomplish even more. After all, that's the point of stretching beyond our known limits. The challenge comes when the knowledge of success drives desire for future success, or the understanding of our capacity to endure hardship causes us to inaccurately assess the impact of future hardship. Essentially, the attitude becomes, "since I handled that, I should be able to handle this." What I believe may happen is that, after enduring much hardship and challenge, we come to believe that our ability to endure future hardship is greater than our actual capacity to endure that hardship. At the beginning of the veteran's career, they are not aware of the limits; they think that their capacity for endurance is much less than it actually is. After experiencing hardship, however, they then begin to achieve much closer than their capacity, and then they still are not aware of their limits, but in the opposite way: they think that their capacity for endurance is much more than it actually is.

A brief illustration from my own career. In the late 1990's, I was stationed at Fort Bragg and served with the 82nd Airborne Division. Among many other things, I jumped out of airplanes. A lot. The last six months I was at Bragg, I jumped eighteen times. Typically, a paratrooper only needs to jump once every three months, but I was trying to get another level of qualification for my Jumpmaster badge. I achieved my goal a week before I left Fort Bragg for my second tour in Germany; of course, there were more immediate repercussions, one of which were four stress fractures that put me on crutches for six months a year after I got to Germany. I truly loved jumping out of airplanes, though, and spent a lot of time in my career trying to get back to it. Ten years after I left Fort Bragg, I came to Fort Carson, Colorado, under the assumption that I would be able to jump again. The

Army had other plans. The possibility of returning to the Airborne community was closed; but six years later, when I was contemplating retirement and considering what life was like after the military, THEN the Army decides to give me what I had been wanting since 1999.

A lot of things changed between 1999 and 2012: not just thirteen years, but three combat tours, and about twenty five pounds. I thought I would jump right back in to where I left off, pun intended; but time, age, and gravity, had other plans, just like the Army did. I used to be able to jump three times a week, but recovering from a jump when you're 25 is much easier than recovering from a jump when you're 38. There was no way that I could have physically endured the pace of jumping that I did in the late '90s, although mentally I both thought I could and wanted to. At 25 years old, my own perceived capacity for hardship was less than my actual capacity; at 38 years old, my perceived capacity for hardship was greater than my actual capacity. It was only after another injury on a jump, and then two more jumps to confirm what I didn't want to admit, did I come to the realization…my jumping days were over.

And yet I still survived. Thrived, even. Some of the most amazing experiences I had in my military career happened in those last three years of working with 10th Special Forces group. All of the stress, all of the pain, was absolutely worth it. Even the life lesson…realizing that I overestimated my capacity for hardship…was invaluable.

If you're working with veterans, and you experience resistance or self-condemnation in them where they think they should be able to handle whatever's going on in their life, understand that they were trained that way. They may not be aware of it. And very often, a veteran's capacity for awareness is actually much more than they think it is.

THE STRENGTH TO BEAR EVIL: LESSONS TO A VETERAN FROM TOLSTOY

Of the things I enjoyed about my military deployments, one of the most unique was: free books.

Wherever I was deployed to around the world, there was always a room, a tent, a building, in which books were donated to be sent overseas to the troops. Inevitably, I always returned from these overseas tours with more books than I went with. I could typically be found browsing through tables and bookshelves full of free literature. I've found hardbound editions of The Three Musketeers printed in the 1940s, and a really neat edition of Crowded Hours by Alice Roosevelt Longworth in the embassy in Mauritania.

One of the most impactful books that I picked up, though, was the one I snagged during my first deployment to Bosnia in 1995: The Forged Coupon, by Leo Tolstoy[1]. This book resonated with me on several different levels at different points in my life, but the main point that I have taken from it has been constant from the first time I read it: ultimate evil is only overcome by someone who is strong enough to absorb it's impact and not pass it on.

If you haven't read it, I highly recommend it. There is no way that I can do it justice with the space I have available here, and it is a pretty short and easy read. Of course, it is a Russian novel, so expect a complicated cast of characters, but the message of human interaction is easily understood.

The story begins small, with a conflict between a father and his son. The father has a bad day at work, and the son is asking for an advance on his allowance, which the father refuses to give; instead, there are insults and bitterness.

The boy owes money to a friend; he asks advice from another friend, who is a less than savory character. This "friend" recommends that they forge the money and pass it off to a local shopkeeper's wife in order to settle the debt. Small crime, yeah? No major issues.

The shopkeeper's wife doesn't notice the con. The shopkeeper does, however, and is angry with his wife…but passes the forged note on to a peasant selling wood. The peasant gets arrested for later passing the forged note, and each wrong is compounded on another, passing the story down the line. The shopkeeper bears false witness against the peasant, a witness to the transaction committed perjury, and is later fired by the shopkeeper for theft. The story continues, passing injustice along from character to character, culminating in horse theft (grand theft auto, in those days), manslaughter, and serial murder.

The culmination of the first half of the book ends when a serial murderer is faced with a victim that does not condemn, but instead asks, "How can you destroy somebody's soul...and worse, your own?" at the precise point of death. That act...being more concerned about his soul that her own life...causes the murderer to repent, be held accountable, and the second half of the book is similar to the first half, only in the other direction. Good deed builds on good deed and is passed on through each of the characters until ending with a reconciliation between the original father and son.

Be advised, there is a large amount of condemnation of what was seen as hypocrisy against organized religion, as Tolstoy wrote this after the Russian Orthodox Church excommunicated him. Not that it's relevant here, but it is pretty on-the-nose in the book.

So great story, right? What is this, a book report? As I mentioned at the beginning, this book had a pretty big influence on my own personal world view. The idea that evil...or anything negative, such as badness, anger, bullying, condemnation...can be stopped by someone strong enough to absorb it, endure it, without passing it on to others. It could be seen as naïve, sure, but let me give you a few examples.

Service members do it, as do other first responders like firefighters and law enforcement. We place ourselves in dangerous situations so that others don't have to. We bear the weight of deployments, we fight and sacrifice, so that others don't have to. There are hundreds of other reasons, to be sure, but the strength in veterans is that they are able to build their strength in order to bear much on behalf of our nation.

Leaders do it, on behalf of their teams. When a crisis happens, or a customer goes on a rampage, a good leader will absorb the impact of the criticism without passing on the frustration, anger, and bitterness to their subordinates. By providing that type of "top cover", the employees are able to address the issue and solve the problem rather than focusing on their own negative feelings. Again, as long as the leader is strong enough, mentally or emotionally, they are able to keep the chain of negativity going.

In my own profession, counselors and therapists most certainly do it. I recently read an amazing blog by another therapist that describes the experience of absorbing what we hear rather than passing it on to those we care about. Doc Warren[1] uses the analogy of John Coffey from the Green Mile[2] and his supernatural ability to remove the pain of others, while still feeling that pain himself.

Don't get me wrong, I'm not talking about suppression or turning a blind eye to bad stuff. I'm talking about addressing the problem in a productive way rather than compounding negativity with negativity and making the situation worse. If injustice is happening, address it appropriately, solve the problem constructively. Those who absorb the evil, offload it in a healthy way, rather than passing it along.

The world is changed by individuals and their relationships, rather than by huge movements. One of the best ways to do this is to absorb negativity without passing it on...we can do with a lot less negative in the world.

THE JOY OF A GOOD PLAN WELL EXECUTED

I'm a child of the '80s. While that may mean many things…yuppies, valley girls, and glam rock…to me that means really awesome TV. To me, MacGyver will always have a mullet, and B.A. Baracus will always pity the fool.

One of my early TV heroes, speaking of old B.A. Baracus, was the indomitable Hannibal Smith, leader of the A-Team[1]. Somehow I never got to be Hannibal when we "played" A-Team, but it was his cunning, ingenuity, and resourcefulness that everyone looked to in order to get the job done. His famous line?

I love it when a plan comes together.

Who doesn't love it when a good plan comes to fruition? I'm sitting in the airport this morning, and we all know that this entails a planning process that starts days, if not weeks, ahead of time. All of the hassles…parking, tickets, boarding passes, bags, security checkpoint, all of that…and much of that is out of your control. Somehow, though, the plan of packing, checking, repacking, online, figuring out transportation on the other end, it all seems to be working out so far. I know, it's not an accomplishment on the level with saving a small town from a pack of renegade outlaw bikers, but hey, I think old Hannibal would be proud.

The key part of Hannibal's statement is not the plan, however…it's the joy that is felt when that plan actually happens. The sense of relief, satisfaction, appreciation that we were actually able to predict, with some level of certainty, that events would unfold as we wanted them to.

Planning is huge for veterans. We love timelines, schedules, and itineraries. Backwards planning is sometimes key for success: figure out when you want something to happen, figure out what steps need to be taken before you get to that point, and work backwards from there. While it's great for military operations, it also works for life…sometimes.

My beautiful and long-suffering wife and I were married in 1999. We got married in her hometown, and parts of my family were able to make it in. Because of the groups of people, we were staying in one hotel, my parents in another, her family was all there…lots of stuff. As she was getting ready, I decided I would be nice and do what a good Noncommissioned Officer does, and create a dual timeline. I started out with the time the wedding was supposed to start, what times we needed to get to our respective families, and worked backwards from there. Proud of my planning ability, I presented this excellent plan to my bride-to-be…who smiled sweetly, crumpled up the paper, and threw it over her shoulder. "Southerners don't do timelines, honey."

One of us made it to the church on time that day, though. Guess which one?

The joke is on me, though…my meticulous planning, my irrelevant timeline, ultimately didn't matter…we still got married that day. And there was joy in that day, just as there is joy in remembering that day.

Think about a time in which you planned a complicated event and it came off. Maybe not perfectly, but it still happened. That sense of joy, of satisfaction, often made the hard work worth it. If it was challenging, how much more fulfilling the success?

Have you ever watched a sunrise? You could have done it this morning. Or yesterday. You have the opportunity to do it tomorrow, God willing. But I remember one particular sunrise, and the sense of satisfaction I enjoyed. In the late '90s, at Fort Bragg, there were thousands of ways to jump out of aircraft; by yourself, with people you didn't know, with people you did know. One of the most common ways, at least in my day, was known as a Mass Tactical operation, six or seven different aircraft kicking out hundreds of paratroopers in the span of thirty minutes or an hour. These jumps usually happened sometime between 2300 (11PM) and 0300 (3AM), a set of hours collectively known as "0-dark-thirty." If you were jumping with your unit, each organization had a rally point on the drop zone; you were supposed to land, collect your equipment, and move tactically to a designated spot on the drop zone to meet up with the rest of your crew. Sometimes there was a follow on mission, if the Commander was feeling tactical, but often it was just a place to gather at the end of the jump. You sit in a circle, parachutes in the middle, leaning back on your rucksack, and break out the smokes while you wait for the rest of the guys. You look left and right at your buddies, they bum one of your smokes, and you both smile while watching the sun rise. Satisfaction in a job well done. Joy when a plan comes together.

Often, plans don't come off the way they were "supposed" to. There is much to be said about making an 80% plan, with 20% flexibility. There were probably a lot of things out of my control this morning that could have derailed my plan to get to the gate on time, and I prepared for that possibility. I built enough time in my plan. Adamantly sticking to a 100% plan at all costs is sometimes as foolish as going in with a 20% plan.

What plans do you have, and what do you need to do to make them happen? Have you figured out your contingencies, analyzed the possibilities, and then stepped forward with boldness?

When you have, remember to take time and recognize the joy in a good plan well executed.

FOR VETERANS, REMEMBERING WHERE YOU CAME FROM IS KEY TO A SUCCESSFUL TRANSITION

There is one aspect of leadership that is key to success…to never forget where you came from. In the context of being a leader, this means to remember what is like when you were a follower, and lead accordingly.

I came to realize that this not only applies to leadership in the hierarchy sense, but also in a temporal way; specifically, in this context it applies to veterans who have transitioned, either out of combat or out of the service. If we remember where we came from, what strength we had when we were in the service, then we can apply that strength to our transition.

See, transition can be a challenging time. It doesn't matter whether you are returning home after a deployment to an active duty military base or returning home to your community after a reserve deployment. You could be leaving the military after six years, sixteen years, or twenty-six years…change is challenging. Moving into the unknown is challenging. Know what, though? For veterans, change is what we did, and change is what we do.

Never forgetting where you came from means that, during your transition, awareness of the strength you relied on in the service can help you apply that strength to whatever challenges you face in the future.

It always amazes me how I can be seemingly impervious to large changes, but small changes drive me out of my mind. Eight houses in ten years? Not a problem. Changing jobs every eighteen months? Got it handled. Change the time the chow hall opens by half an hour, though, and it's as if the whole world came crashing down; close down your favorite gate getting on post, and the entire day is thrown in the trash. Why are we able to weather the hurricanes of change with strength and resolve, but a little rainstorm knocks us off our game? Maybe it's because we don't apply the same determination and acceptance to both experiences.

Consider the transitions that you encountered while in the service. New duty station. New superiors. The young private meeting the Platoon Sergeant for the first time, the young Lieutenant being greeted by their Squadron Commander. There was trepidation there, right? Maybe some anxiety, and anxiousness to please, the fear of screwing up? You got through it, though. Maybe you messed up, maybe you didn't…but it didn't kill you. You learned that you were able to bear a lot more than you thought you could. And that kept happening, experience after experience, for as long as you were in the service.

How about now, though? The trepidation, the uncertainty of transition…is that the same feeling you had when you got orders in your hand for a new base or billet? If you were able to handle it then, why is now difficult? Some of it does have to do with the fact that we are familiar with what we know, but uncomfortable with a disruption in our routine.

I talk to veterans often who talk about the familiarity of their deployments. From the largest Forward Operating Base to the smallest Combat Outpost, you came to know your camp like the back of your hand. You knew when chow was served, you knew which was the best shower to go to at the best time. Mail arrived in the afternoon, you could always catch you supervisor at this time or that time. Life was predictable, except when it wasn't…and even that sometimes seemed to follow a pattern.

Compare that to coming back home, or leaving the service. The predictable routine has changed. What we knew is no longer what we know. I experienced this myself; on my deployment to Iraq, I was the company Operations NCO, one of four decision makers in the unit along with the Commander, his Executive Officer, and the First Sergeant. Over 160 Soldiers, and if one of the four of us said that something needed to be done, it happened. When I came home on mid-tour leave, however, I certainly didn't carry the same weight! Regardless of how much I tried to make it be so, my wife didn't listen to me, my kids didn't listen to me, the cats wouldn't even listen to me. It took some serious reflection on my part…and some direct communication from my amazing and supportive wife…to make me aware that my role had changed. I had the adaptability to respond to different situations in the service, why did I have such a hard time responding to different situations out of the service? Because I forgot where I came from. I forgot the strengths and ability that I had developed and cultivated in the Army.

If you once believed something to be a beneficial truth in your life, then it will always remain a truth, even if you later think it is a lie.

When I was in the military, I was confident. I was able. The truth that I knew was that, with the proper focus and planning, I could train my platoon or my company, within the Commander's intent, to get the job done. The truth that I knew was, at it's core, "I Can" and "I'm Capable." Why then, during a transition, I believe that truth to be a lie? Why do I change "can" to "can't" and "will" to "won't?" Because I forgot where I came from.

There are many levels of challenges that we face when we return from deployments, or transition out of the military. We are truly entering unchartered waters…but isn't that we did six years ago, or sixteen, or twenty-six? We survived, and even thrived, then, what's to say we can't do it now?

If you are a veteran, remember where you came from. For your own sake. And when you get to where you are going because you relied on what you knew, turn around and help your brother and sister. Mutual support both to and from our buddies on the right and left is how we made it through the service, and that same mutual support is how we are going to not only survive after the service, but thrive.

MILITARY TRANSITION: JUMPING OUT OF A PLANE IN THE FOG

In late 1999, at Fort Bragg, North Carolina, I jumped out of an airplane in the fog.

Through the quirks of assignments during a 22 year Army career, I've only had the pleasure of two Airborne assignments out of eight or nine different ones. Those two were three years as a paratrooper with the 82nd in the late 90s, and the last years of my career in the 10th Special Forces Group support element. Throughout those two assignments, I conducted something like 35 or 36 jumps. To be honest, nearing retirement, I lost count, and my 35 jumps are nowhere near the number of many career-long paratroopers. Many of those jumps blur together, but this was one that still sticks with me to this day.

I don't remember the exact date, although I know it was sometime in the fall. We knew that the weather conditions were going to be less than ideal, because we had been briefed that the aircraft pilots were going to be using the Adverse Weather Arial Delivery System[1] (AWADS), a system that allows the pilots to know when to release personnel, equipment, and supplies during weather conditions that preclude visual confirmation of release points on the ground.

This jump was memorable because it was unlike any jump that I had ever made before, or any jump I made after that. When I exited the aircraft, there were several things I could remember. First, total and absolute silence, almost a complete peace. I felt as if I were the only paratrooper in the air, which is a hard feat to accomplish after exiting a C130...usually the entire sky around you is filled with your fellow airborne brethren. Second, near zero visibility. I could see my parachute above me as a round shadow, and the ground below me as an even larger shadow. Third, the air around me seemed to be glowing, thanks to the full moon that could barely be seen as a bright disk somewhere up above. Coupled with the fact that we were released at a much higher altitude than our typical 800 feet above ground level, and I felt as though I was floating through a surreal dream world forever. Of course, the landing still had to happen.

This experience can be correlated to transitioning out of the military. Typically, most veterans only leave the military once; the exceptions, of course, are those who got out, came back in, and left the service again, but for the majority of veterans I work with, once was enough.

We jumped out of the airplane, you and I. Whether we were ready for it or not, whether our heart, our mind, or our finances were in the right place, we still jumped. One of the first things I realized when I transitioned was how strangely alone I felt. The airplane kept flying…the Army kept going. As I was heading towards my retirement, I was talking to my company leadership about needing to take some time to transition, and they said, "no problem, take all the time you need."

"Wait a minute," I said, "I do a lot of stuff around here, I need to make sure that things are handed off the right way."

"You're right, you sure do…and it will either happen or not happen when you leave. We'll figure it out."

As on that fall night over Sicily Drop Zone, I felt alone. Didn't seem like there was anyone else in the air around me. Our TAP[2] class at Fort Carson had a wide range of soldiers attending, from junior enlisted soldiers to Senior NCOs and Officers. Each of us had different goals, different agendas, different ideas about what was coming next…and each of us felt as though we were in the sky by ourselves.

Like on that jump, I was entering into unknown territory. I had zero visibility; I was jumping into a fog. I knew nothing about resumes, interviews, dressing for success; even figuring out how to transition to bi-weekly paychecks rather than twice a month was a challenge. I had my intended career path, as I was already a year and a half into my Master's Degree, but I had no clue how I was going to bridge the gap between retirement and graduation.

However, both with the jump and with transition, there was one inevitable thing: regardless of how alone or connected I felt, or how much visibility I had, I was going to land sooner or later. I was going to hit the ground, I was going to be out of the military. Once I hit the ground, it was my choice to lay there and wait for something to happen, or get up and make something happen. Everything began and ended with my own choice.

All of this is about our outlook. Our mindset. I could have been scared out of my wits that night, and (to tell you the truth) there was a bit of fear there. My excitement, however, my outlook, had a lot to do with overcoming that fear. I trusted in my equipment. I trusted in the professionals that helped me prepare that equipment. I trusted the pilots that released us over the correct drop zone. I found myself with moments of doubt during my transition, too. I trusted my equipment there, as well; I followed the advice of those who had jumped out of the plane before me, and made my own luck happen where luck didn't seem to be around much.

If you find yourself struggling in your transition, remind yourself: I'm not alone in the sky. Even though I have zero visibility, I trust in my equipment. And it's been one hell of a ride.

COMPLIMENT OR CRITICISM, KEVLAR OR VELCRO?

I have yet to find the man, however exalted his station, who did not do better work and put forth greater effort under a spirit of approval than under a spirit of criticism. Charles Schwab

"Hey, the Commander wants to see you."

"@#%$, what now?"

"I don't know, but he looked pissed."

Sound familiar? Replace "Commander" with any authority figure at any level, whether it be "Gunny" or "Smoke" or "Chief", and you'll get the same effect. In our time in the military, we learn to react a certain way when things like this happen, and in my experience it has never been positive. Has this caused you to develop emotional Kevlar[1], or emotional Velcro?

Think about the Kevlar lining in your body armor, flak jacket, whatever. It's not completely bulletproof, but it is significantly resilient enough to stop small shrapnel and sharp objects. Compare that to the Velcro on that body armor…it's a magnet for all kinds of the crap that floats around in the air. Which of the two did you have to spend more time cleaning when it came time to turn in your gear?

We can get the same way emotionally and psychologically. Sometimes, the stuff we hear bounces off our mind like a pebble bouncing off our body armor, and other times, the stuff we hear attaches to our minds like military-grade adhesive. The problem is, we often let the bad stuff stick, and allow the good stuff to bounce off.

Like many veterans, I'm not very good at compliments or appreciation. When someone says I did a good job at something, I shift the compliment to someone else or dismiss it with, "I was only doing my job, I'm not special at all." Criticism, though, I can certainly take that one to the bank. Which was more impactful to you, a positive performance review or a negative one? If that was the case when you were in the military, have you carried it into life as well?

The specificity of the compliment or criticism is important. When we receive compliments, we need to know exactly what it was about the action being complimented that was "good"…saying "you did a good job, there" is not enough to make it stick to our emotional Velcro. We need to know why you thought it was a good job, what about the job was good, how good it was compared to other jobs that were done, and most of the time, we will STILL deny that it was a good job because we don't want to be seen as an arrogant jerk! How about the details of the criticism, though? We certainly don't need those! When someone tells us, "you sure screwed that one up", we take that particular ball and run with it without checking to see if it's even our ball to take! Without taking as hard a look at criticism as we do with compliments, we would not be able to dispute it. It's a forgone conclusion…yep, I screwed up, won't happen again. Meanwhile, we walk away kicking ourselves in the fourth point of contact, likely for something that wasn't entirely our fault to begin with.

Don't get me wrong. I'm huge on personal responsibility and being accountable for my own actions, and recommend a healthy dose of personal accountability for everyone. The problem is, a lot of the veterans I meet are carrying a load of personal accountability that is greater than they should. We all have moments in our past where we think, "that's my fault." It's the nature of the work that we did; serious, critical, life-changing stuff. The word "fault", though, implies guilt, which is one of those words that attaches to our emotional Velcro, and won't come off unless we do a whole bunch of scrubbing.

The source of the compliment and criticism is also important. Some random yahoo who we don't even know, when THEY say, "you sure jacked that one up, pal," we don't even give it the time of day. Bounces off the emotional Kevlar like a rock from a slingshot. The problem is, a compliment from the same random yahoo also bounces off without impact. Criticism from a trusted source…a valued mentor, one of our subordinates, a spouse or a parent? Buckle up, because we're taking that one all the way down the road. We will attach it to our emotional Velcro and leave it on so long that it's like it was applied with 100MPH tape[2]. Compliments received from a thousand random yahoos will not counteract one criticism from someone close to us. Many times, we will weed through those hundred compliments just to find the one criticism, then say, "Hah! See? I was right! I DID jack it up." Then we walk down the road kicking ourselves in the fourth point of contact. See a pattern?

"You have been criticizing yourself for years and it hasn't worked. Try approving of yourself and see what happens." Louise L. Hay

What about the compliments and criticism that we give to ourselves? Forget the fact that we are our own worst critics and are unlikely to compliment ourselves in the general sense anyway. The criticism that we tell ourselves sticks to our emotional Velcro quicker, stronger, and longer than any amount of criticism that others can give. We continue to punch ourselves in the face long after the fight is over…why is that? Do we enjoy feeling like crap, struggling with guilt, shame, transforming it into anger and bitterness like some dysfunctional alchemist? I don't know about you, but I sure don't like feeling like that, and most veterans I work with don't enjoy it either. So why do we do it to ourselves?

The key is awareness; being aware of how you react to criticism, and how you react to compliments. You don't have to stand on top of the mountain and shout to the world that you're the greatest…ain't none of us Mohammad Ali (unless you are Mohammad Ali, and on LinkedIn, and choose to randomly read this post and comment, which would be amazing). At the same time, though, you don't have to deflect compliments as if they were criticism, and accept criticism as though they were compliments. Give each of them equal value, considering the source, and allow yourself the opportunity to appreciate each of them. Swap them around…for compliments, use less Kevlar and more Velcro, and for criticism, use less Velcro and more Kevlar. You might find that the balance you obtain will lead to a more pleasant and fulfilling life.

LIVING LIFE LOOKING THROUGH A VETERAN FILTER

As I was on my way to the airport recently, I looked out the window and was instantly transported to a moment seen years ago. I'm not talking about a flashback but a faint temporary double vision, a memory of the past overlaid on the reality of the present.

In the distance, past a wide field surrounding the airport, was a line of low industrial buildings that surround many American airports today. The morning sky was grey, threatening a storm later or maybe the remnant of a storm past. In the near distance, just over the line of industrial buildings, was a tightly clenched fist of black smoke. A fire or some other calamity, perhaps, or the sign of the exhaust of a huge piece of heavy machinery starting up. The driver of our cab, and the other passengers in the back, didn't think twice, didn't comment or even interrupt their conversation.

I was instantly reminded of an incident in June of 2009, while in Jalalabad Air Field in Regional Command East, Afghanistan; in my memory, that tight fist of black smoke was the remnant of a controlled detonation of a recently discovered cache of unauthorized explosives and munitions outside the base. When a pile of explosives is located, military specialists usually use their own explosives to destroy the find, in what is known as a "controlled det." As a matter of fact, as I looked over to my right and saw the cloud, that exact phrase leapt into my mind: Controlled Det[1].

Everyone has their own lived experience that they bring with them to any situation. Our childhood influences our values. Our past failures induce our future fears. Our successes give confidence.

Military veterans, whether they have deployed to combat or not, have their experiences overlay the present. While some of it has to do with sights or sounds that bring about an automatic physical response, it also has to do with triggers of memory or habitual modes of thought that lead to repeated behaviors. I didn't experience any type of automatic fear response when I saw that black smoke: my heart rate didn't rise, I didn't become short of breath. My muscles didn't clinch and my hair didn't stand on end…but I can almost guarantee that I was the only one of the four of us that had that thought when I saw that smoke.

The feeling of seeing the world through a Veteran filter continued for the rest of the morning. Patience at the hurry-up-and-wait security lines, not an issue because of frequent in-and-out of airports while in the military caused me to pad my timeline. My bemusement at the staffer behind the ticket counter who seemed, inexplicably, to have never seen a military retiree ID card and brightly asked me if I were in the Marines, despite the U.S. Army pin clearly on my lapel.

A conversation I had with a young Soldier going through the airport on his way home on leave to be there in time to see the birth of his daughter. He was very respectful and polite (a "public persona" that is often used by veterans and service members, quite different from who we are around our buddies), and who was almost ashamed to explain that he was on his way home from Kuwait, but was not able to deploy to Iraq or Afghanistan. We talked about his uncles who had deployed to combat, who had told him that it was "lots of fun" and his current leaders who often talk about "the good old deployments." I could see the respect he had on his face for his uncles and his leaders, and sense his regret at not being able to join them…and absolutely relate, having once been there myself. I did hand him my business card, which he took politely, but also confusedly…what would he do with a business card? Something like that could be as unfamiliar to a young Soldier as an entrenching tool or a P38 is to someone who has never served.

Even airplanes, the act of travelling, remind me of flights in the past: freedom birds away from overseas deployments, trans-Atlantic flights back and forth from tours in Germany. Airplanes that took off with me in them, and landed without me because I jumped out of them halfway through. A rich, varied, jumbled group of memories obtained from decades in the military. Sometimes memories will be recalled deliberately, taken from a stockpile of stories that never seem to wear out (for us at least) and sometimes memories that pop up out of nowhere like a sudden thunderstorm on a later summer afternoon.

The view from the veteran filter is often helpful for us. Many veterans I know are creative problem solvers who know how to do much with little. If fully aware of our capabilities, we can take advantage of our varied experiences and lend a different perspective on a situation. We can weigh consequences of our decisions fairly rapidly, if not always accurately, because the consequences of our decisions while we were in the military were often significant, and we understood the magnitude of success and failure.

Mostly, I feel, our capacity for endurance is greater. Once you've been through a firestorm, a warm day doesn't bother you. Everyone's reaction to stressful experiences is subjective; if I were to ask you to rate your level of anger on a scale from one to ten, the 10 on your scale would necessarily need to be the angriest you've ever been. Same with fear. Joy, even. Your maximum level of fear, however, may only be at a five on my own personal subjective scale, or vice versa based on your lived experience. For me, viewing life through my veteran filter helps to calm me, as I think to myself, "At least…" As bad as this is, at least it's not combat. As boring as this is, at least it's not the sheer utter boredom of being stuck on an outpost with nothing but a pack of cards.

We each have filters that we view the world through. For veterans, that filter is just a little more…interesting.

FOR VETERANS, A REST PLAN IS CRITICAL TO FUTURE SUCCESS

"Every person needs to take one day away. A day in which one consciously separates the past from the future. Jobs, family, employers, and friends can exist one day without any one of us, and if our egos permit us to confess, they could exist eternally in our absence. Each person deserves a day away in which no problems are confronted, no solutions searched for. Each of us needs to withdraw from the cares which will not withdraw from us."— Maya Angelou

Take a knee, drink water. How many times have you heard that during your military service? On a range, during a march? Hydration is key. If you're like me, slightly old-school, you remember the old Lister Bag[1], which was replaced by the ubiquitous Water Buffalo[2], and augmented by the Water Tanker and the even cooler Hippo[3]. Ensuring that we had the ability to marshal our strength and replenish our depleted energy was key to continued mission success.

How tired were you after a day at the range? Or a ten, twelve, twenty mile ruck march? One of my most satisfying personal accomplishments is being known as "that bald @#$!(*& that made us ruck in a blizzard." Built character, though, and some are still talking about it. I made sure, however, that when we got back to the motor pool, we had hot chow and coffee waiting. Why? Because the rest after strenuous effort somehow seems more restorative than just lying around.

One of the most interesting things that I found about the human body is that rarely, in times of extreme stress and required activity, do we notice more basic biological urges. I don't recall being hungry, tired, or needing to go to the bathroom when I was in the middle of a firefight. When I was pulling Jumpmaster[4] duties, I don't recall needing to take a leak or a nap…but after the mission or the jump was over, get out of my way. Getting into base after a mission, all you wanted to do was hit the latrine, the dining facility, and the rack, not necessarily in that order and as quickly as possible.

What about now, though? After all, we are no longer pulling missions, or shifts, or conducting patrols. How important is taking a knee and drinking water in our civilian lives? I mean, being a hard charger, that's what success meant in the military, and being a hard charger in our new endeavor is the way to success, right?

100% accurate, right up to the point where we faceplant in the front yard because we drove ourselves too far without taking a break.

Were we really always hard charging when we were in? Wasn't there block leave, and Training Holidays, and scheduled time off? Even after 24 hour

Staff Duty or CQ[5], we got the next day off. It sucked, sure, but we had the time to recover. We knew what would happen if we drove ourselves and our troops too long, too far, and too hard. We might have gotten away with it when we were in the field, or on a huge training event, but there was no way we could have done it longer than 72 hours. Absolutely, we pushed our physical and mental limits, but it was not continuous, and there was a period of rest at the end of it.

Don't get me wrong, I'm the first guy to admit that I haven't taken a real vacation since returning from Afghanistan in 2012, and that was only because I hadn't signed into my new unit yet. Any leave that I took before my retirement was geared towards school activities, and I was already working when I was on terminal leave. Even when I am not working at my regular job, I am doing some other kind of work. Somehow, I think that I'm not alone here…to be idle, to rest, for many veterans is a form of wastefulness. We feel productive when we DO stuff, and "lazy" when we are NOT doing stuff.

Do you give yourself time to recover now? Is the stress of the job search and the level of uncertainty about the future driving you to do more? Do we feel that we constantly need to drive forward in our relentless pursuit of whatever our goal is? How often do we reach a goal we previously set, and are already looking towards the horizon? It's as if we keep moving the finish line for ourselves.

I am in no way advocating total capitulation to a sedentary lifestyle. I couldn't in good conscience sell that idea, and you wouldn't buy it anyway. But do we need to always suck it up, drive on, carry on, and push through the pain? I did that several times in my military career, and have the cracked legs and compressed back to prove it. The problem is, many of us think that we are so critical to the mission that it will fail if we're not standing at our post. It's not arrogance, it's that we understand the importance of what we did and what we are doing, and the only way that we feel as though we can ensure complete success is to do the darn thing ourselves.

My last day on active duty was 31 July, 2014. Do you know what happened on August 1st on Fort Carson? Reveille sounded, every unit on post held formation, the Army kept going. I know, I checked. Not that I felt as though I was critical to the operation of the entire United States Army, but to remind myself that I am simply a veteran now. My wars have been fought, my time has been served. That's true after twenty-two years, and it would have been true if it had only been two years.

The challenges at work will always be there. You can either relentlessly pursue them and burn out like a shooting star, or take the time to give yourself a break, both literally and figuratively, and continue to shine.

How do you rest? What do you do to recharge your batteries, in what way do you now take a knee and drink water? We made sure our troops did it while we were in...why do we avoid doing it now?

VETERANS AND THE DESTRUCTIVE POWER OF EXPLOSIVES

Veterans are good at blowing stuff up.

For most veterans, blowing stuff up is a skill that is taught in basic training. How to throw a grenade. How to place a Claymore mine[1]. How to fire an AT4, a shoulder-mounted rocket[2]. For some veterans, their occupational specialty taught them how to handle ordnance and explosives, to build them and employ them and use them for stuff. Just the right amount of explosives can open a locked door, or take down the entire building.

Before anyone who reads this gets offended at a celebration of violence and destruction, that's part of what being in the military is about. I don't mean to say that all veterans gleefully employ destructive means to accomplish simple tasks, but the truth is that the purpose of the military is to fight and win our Nation's wars. That can't be done with rocks and sticks.

The problem with explosives is, sometimes they can get us into trouble. Way back in the mid '90s, a team of us went to Norway on a mission to support a joint NATO exercise. A friend of mine introduced me to the awesomeness that is an "MRE Bomb." The rations that service members are given, Meals Ready to Eat (MREs), come with a flameless heater that uses a chemical reaction that is activated by water to heat the meal. By crushing up some MRE heaters, putting it in a bottle, adding water, and putting the cap on, the escaping gasses will expand to the point where it will cause the bottle to explode with a loud but harmless noise.

Our tent was located at the back of an area that had been plowed clear, and was up against a snow berm that must have been eight or ten feet tall. After putting a couple of these MRE Bombs together, my buddy and I threw them over the snow berm to wait for the explosion; we got our explosion, all right, but what we didn't know what that the motorpool for the Norwegian Army was on the other side. We figured out pretty quick, though, by the sounds of shouting and running and yelling.

Another interesting fact about the military: punishments can be just as creative as the transgressions that cause them. Have you seen the guy at the airport with the cone flashlights guiding the airplane? They need that for helicopter landing zones, too. Especially at midnight. In the snow. Twenty miles south of the Arctic Circle. Needless to say, we didn't make any more MRE bombs on that particular trip.

Fun stories and inventive punishments aside, destruction is something that veterans are good at. The majority of us don't handle live ordnance or explosives after we leave the military, but we often do sabotage our lives by metaphorically blowing stuff up.

A mentor of mine once described our emotions as bottles and jars in a cabinet, but anger is the one jar that we shook up and sprayed all over the other emotions. It has been variously described as a cork, a method of control over ourselves and our environment, and a blanket. Whatever metaphor you'd like to use, anger is another thing that veterans are good at, and the literal destructive power of explosives partners well with the figurative destructive power of anger.

Many of the veterans I work with find themselves in situations where they feel as though they need to throw a figurative grenade and walk away. School not going the way we'd like? @#%$ it, I'm done. Didn't really want to do it anyway. Job too much of a hassle? Pop a grenade, I'm outta here. Relationship not working out? Fine. Drop a thermite grenade and watch it burn (figuratively, of course).

The problem is, when we do this too often, all we see around us is the shattered remains of our destructive tendencies. Looking around at a destroyed wasteland makes us angrier, which causes a downward spiral of pain and loss, leading to more frustration, anger, and depression.

There is a time and a place for explosives, and it's not in our post-military lives. Solving problems in this way can be debilitating to both ourselves and those around us. The challenge is that when we are in the emotional state to want to use figurative explosives in our lives, we are less likely to use rational, conscious measures to figure out the problem. If school isn't working out, then maybe we're not going after the right degree. If work is a challenge, we don't have to rage quit, we can figure out a different way to engage or, if it's still not working out, to disengage. And if our relationships are not working out the way we expect them to, an honest look at our own actions and the dynamics between us and our partner is a much better way of solving whatever problems there are than just blowing the relationship up.

If you're a veteran, and you've had some challenges in your post-military life, it may be helpful to take a good look at how you address those challenges. Are you throwing a grenade and walking away, explosions in the background like some Hollywood war flick? Sure, there are times when we want to do that, it's a fantasy response. Urges are okay, as long as you don't act upon them if they are harmful to yourself or others. But taking the time to understand how we approach these problems, and solving them in a more deliberate and less destructive way, can give us the stability we are looking for.

Who we were is no longer who we are, and we can leave the bullets and bombs in the past, where they belong.

VETERANS, CHOOSE TO FILL SPACE IN YOUR LIFE, OR HAVE IT FILLED FOR YOU

A significant challenge that veterans face during transition is they find that there is a wide open space in front of them. We can either choose how we fill that space, or it will be filled for us.

The options are seemingly endless, but there are limits. Limits to our abilities, limits to our finances, the choices of geographical location. Perhaps we move back home to family, or stay at our final duty station. Maybe we take the opportunity to start over and end up in a new place that we've never been. While the choices are not limitless, however, the limits are so far on the horizon that it certainly appears to be so. Sometimes, when that happens, we can experience paralysis through analysis.

The fact is, though, that life is going to continue. The earth is going to continue to turn, the sun and the moon are going to traverse the sky, and we need to do something. We can either give up control and let life happen, or we can start to make choices and make life happen.

You can choose to fill up the empty space in your career after the service, or it will be filled up for you. Letting it be filled up for you is to grab the first job that comes along that pays the bills, and staying with that even though you don't enjoy it. You are not limited by your experience, and certainly not by your job in the military. It may be tough to get into another industry, but not impossible. Allow me to illustrate.

When I joined the Army, I enlisted in the Reserves. I chose a job in logistics, Motor Transport Operator (euphemistically) or Truck Driver (reality). Through a series of circumstances…the Reserves did not have Combat Arms positions, the strange and seemingly insignificant fact (up until that point) that I didn't seem to see colors the same way as other people, and the fact that I wanted to take the first thing smoking out of town…my job choices were limited. When I joined Active Duty a year later, I was told that I couldn't change my job, and (again) wanting to take the first thing smoking out of town, I stayed with what I knew. So I spent twenty-two years in Logistics in the Army.

There are some really great jobs in the Logistics industry. Peers of mine have gotten good jobs as fleet managers, warehouse supervisors, route managers. For me, though, it's not what I wanted to do, even though that would have been a comparatively easy route. Instead, I chose to fill the space in my life with something that gave me meaning and purpose: using my military experience and my education in clinical mental health counseling in order to become a therapist for other veterans. Was it easy? Of course not. It took eight years of school, from an Associates to a

Masters, and that time included four deployments and a retirement. It took a lot of sacrifice on my part and my family's part, and some interim choices had to be made. The ultimate goal, however, was to get to a place to help other veterans, and that made the challenge worth it.

You can choose to deliberately fill your emotional space, or that will be filled up for you, too. I don't shout at the TV or the news much…all it does is keep me irritated and it doesn't change what's being put out there. Shaking my fist at the sky will eventually make me tired and the sky will still be there. Why get angry and frustrated at things beyond our control? It is, by definition, out of our control, so why bother to try to control it, unless we enjoy exercises in futility? I don't know about you, but I certainly had enough of that when I was in the military. What we CAN control is how we react to a situation. We can literally choose to smile rather than to frown, to laugh rather than to cry, to believe rather than to doubt. If you think, "no we can't," I challenge you to try it. The "can't" word is one that imposes false limits on the horizon.

The time in our lives is going to be filled up one way or another. There is certainly a period of time after we get out of the service where we think, "now what?" That time will be filled…maybe it's blowing off steam (and money), maybe it's drinking too much. Maybe you find yourself sitting on a beach or standing on a golf course, a dream that you've been aiming at for years, just to find out that the reality of the beach or the golf course doesn't quite seem to match up to the dream. Maybe you find yourself working a dead-end job that doesn't quite give you the satisfaction you had while you were in. Maybe you find yourself working a job with great opportunities, but STILL does not give you that satisfaction. Gotta pay the bills, I understand. With two teenagers rapidly and inevitably headed towards college, I know the feeling. I can choose, however, how I react to the situation, determine the goal that I want to achieve, and conduct backwards planning from there.

We have both less control over our lives, and more control. Less control than we want, and more control than we think. Finding that sweet spot between the two levels of control, and deliberately taking advantage of that gap, will lead to a greater sense of purpose and meaning in our lives.

THE FALLIBILITY...AND HUMANITY...OF VETERANS

As I look back on some of what I have written, I get the sense that I could be giving the impression that all military service members are strong, capable, infallible heroes striding through the modern battlefield fighting for truth, justice, and the American Way. That simply by serving their country, veterans somehow become this awe-inspiring model of virtue and morality.

Nothing could be further from the truth.

If looking at myself in the mirror didn't throw this theory in the garbage, certainly incidents like My Lai[1] and Abu Ghraib[2] convince me that veterans are not virtuous angels whose actions are simply misunderstood and will eventually stand on the right side of history.

I am sure that many veterans like myself can think someone they served with that acted less than professionally, to put it mildly. It would not be accurate to create the impression that the modern military is a place of peace and harmony, where everyone gets along and fairness and equality rule the day. This ain't a recruiting poster, and it's not propaganda with a multitude of smiling Soldiers march off to save the day. If I were trying to paint that picture, I would not point out how prevalent toxic leadership is in today's military. I would not mention the overwhelming and obvious fact that sexual harassment and assault is so widespread. The stigma against mental health would not exist at all in this idealized and sanitized version of the military, so there would be no need for me to write about it.

I don't feel as though it serves any purpose to perpetuate the myth of a Virtuous Warrior, mainly because I know that it's not true. The things that veterans have seen and experienced sometimes make it even more likely that they are less virtuous. Military service in general, and experiencing combat in particular, can cause a veteran to somehow lose focus on their core beliefs about right and wrong, good and bad; this is a key component to the concept of moral injury.

My point here is that veterans are human, and humans are fallible. We make mistakes, and sometimes they're big ones. Sometimes the mistakes are crimes, and calling a crime a mistake is not a way to absolve responsibility, but to understand that there are times in our lives when we fail.

I once read an article that describes the fact that the Army is investigating the allegation that Command Sergeant Major Basil Plumley, the CSM of 1/7 Cav during the Ia Drang campaign, wore decorations that he did not earn[3]. CSM Plumley was the unit Sergeant Major during the events described in the book We Were Soldiers Once...and Young[4], memorably played by Sam Elliott in the movie. A historian has uncovered evidence that

CSM Plumley may have inflated his service record and presented himself as earning commendations and awards that he did not.

To many veterans, nothing gets the blood pumping more than accusations of "stolen valor." The idea that someone would claim to have earned something they didn't, especially if they claimed to have served in the military and hadn't done so, is so distasteful to a veteran that they have lobbied to get legislation passed to make it a crime. But how then do we view veterans who served honorably, in many aspects and according to many accounts, and also made mistakes?

We view them accurately: as humans, who are fallible, but also to be respected for their fallibility and humanity. And we remember them as such, with forgiveness; we can choose to memorialize an idealized version of the truth or we can choose to memorialize the truth. In spite of his fallibility, on a November day in 1965, Basil Plumley earned a Silver Star for his actions on LZ X-Ray.

The key here is forgiveness. Many veterans struggle with the concept of forgiveness. Does the idea that such a respected Soldier as CSM Plumley exaggerated his awards cause you to lose respect for him? Or do the transgressions of General Petreaus in his personal life overshadow the amazing accomplishments in his military career? If the negative somehow tarnishes the positive, could not the positive untarnish some of the negative? If the allegations are true, then I, for one, can choose the path of forgiveness. Not so much for the memory and legacy of CSM Plumley, but for myself. Is being angry or disgusted so pleasant that I need to feel as much of it as I can, as often as I can?

On Memorial Day, we honor those who have sacrificed their lives in the service of our country. I don't know about you, but I know that I'm not perfect, and some of those brothers and sisters that I've lost were not perfect either. Their lack of perfection, their fallibility, in no way diminishes their sacrifice…unless I choose to allow it to.

Others have written about the dangers of negative self-perception, the need to compare ourselves to others. How much worse does that happen when we have a skewed perception of the perfection of others? We are nowhere near as imperfect as we believe, and others are nowhere as perfect as we think they are. Keeping this awareness in mind will keep balance in our lives.

Personally, I hope the allegations against CSM Plumley are not true. If they are true, however, it does not change my respect for him, and does not diminish what I know of his service. Apart from CSM Plumley and General Moore, my personal favorite individual involved in Ia Drang campaign was

Rick Rescorla; on Memorial Day, I will choose to remember him as he was in 1965, leading his Soldiers in combat, and on September 11th, 2001…as others were evacuating the World Trade Center, Rick was going UP the towers, towards the danger rather than away from it[5]. Any sins, any transgressions, any mistakes that he made between those two actions would not diminish the respect that I have for those two actions, nearly 37 years apart to the day…and if I can do that for the "icons" and the "famous", I can do it for my brothers and sisters. And if I can forgive my brothers and sisters for their fallibility, then I can forgive myself for the same.

THE THINGS THEY CARRY NOW

Even before joining the Army, Tim O'Brien's The Things They Carried[1] was a powerful read; going back and looking at it now, from the other side of military life, is even more meaningful.

In a further attempt to help keep the awareness of veteran mental health in the conversation, I thought I might go through what, in my experience, veterans carry today. This won't be anything close to what Tim O'Brien writes, and it's not a half-hearted attempt at flattery disguised as imitation, but it might be intriguing to you.

The main things that veterans today carry are names...the names of places. A lot of those names are well known: Baghdad, Ramadi, Kabul, Kandahar. They are places from less well-known deployments: Slavonski Brod, for example. They are even names from deployments long past, some slightly well known, such as Chosin Reservoir and the Ia Drang Valley, and some not very well known at all. Veterans carry the names of the places they lived, such as FOB Rustamiyah, Camp Leatherneck, OP Bari Ali. They carry the names of the places they fought: the Arghandab Valley, the Dora Market. Sometimes the names of the places they lived were also the names of the places they fought...COP Keating, Wanat, USS Cole.

Veterans carry the names of their units: The All American Division, The Screaming Eagles. Sky Soldier. The Big Red One. They carry the names of their mascots (both approved and unapproved) as both badges of honor and targets of scorn. They carry the names of their operations: Desert Saber (First Gulf War ground campaign), Hastings (Vietnam, '66), Anaconda (Afghanistan, '02). They carry these names in their thoughts, hanging on their walls, tattooed on their skin, in their dreams.

Most of all, veterans carry the names of the men and women they served with. The ones who made it back, and definitely the ones who didn't. They carry with them the names of the battle buddies who did make it back, and then didn't. I know veterans who are younger than thirty years old, with multiple deployments, who have lost more buddies since getting back from combat that they did during combat...and they carry that with them, too.

They carry memories with them. Memories they want to keep forever, memories they want to keep away forever, and painful memories that they never want to forget. Veterans carry the weight of their experiences, of which there are many, and which are heavy. Sometimes, sharing those burdens...sharing those memories...can make them seem less heavy, for a time.

If you know a veteran who is struggling, help them find a counselor or therapist that they can connect with. If it doesn't work out the first time, keep looking, because when it finally does happen, all of the time searching will be worth it.

What names are you carrying? Share with others those words you are still carrying with you, whether it has been three years, thirty years, or fifty years. Chances are, you'll find someone who is carrying the same thing…and your veteran world will grow just a little more connected.

CORRELATION AND CAUSATION: MILITARY SERVICE AND KILLING MACHINES

Let's get the "Killing Machine" argument out of the way. I don't know about you, but I have successfully refrained from engaging in cold-blooded pre-meditated murder after I left the service, and I have twenty-two years of service and three combat tours.

It is human nature to fear what we don't understand, and to dehumanize an individual in order to make neat explanations for what we already think we know. By saying, All _____ are _____, we are creating a bias in our own minds that we then act on as fact. To begin with, the absolutes of "all" and "are" will get us in trouble, because we start to believe it. We believe the exception becomes the rule, because that then allows us to give ourselves the answer to the question everyone wants to know the answer to: "Why?"

When incidents like what happened in Dallas, Texas on 7 July 2016[1] take place, and a veteran is involved, the impulse is to look to the individual's military service as a reason for their actions, essentially claiming that the military creates "killing machines" that are heartless, soulless monsters that are simply focused on destruction.

There is much to be said about military training. It instills discipline. It builds confidence. And yes, it does teach us to overcome our basic fears and aversions in order to accomplish the mission, whether that mission is to attack or defend. It teaches us to "take out the enemy" in a myriad of unique and specialty-specific ways. What it also does is provide a framework in which to use those specific skills, and a certain kind of morality and discernment about when to use those skills and when not to use them.

Military training also instills the ability to appropriately identify who the enemy is, and who it is not.

There is a basic concept in statistics that is taught in just about every entry-level course, and has been reiterated in nearly every psychology course I have ever taken: correlation does not mean causation[2]. Just because two variables are connected does not necessarily mean that one event caused the other. An extreme example is the following statement: "as ice cream sales increase, the rate of _____ increases sharply. Therefore, ice cream consumption causes _____." Replace the blank with what you'd like…homicides, shark attacks, drowning deaths, and you have great example of correlation and causation. Rather than what could be seen as the obvious variable…hot weather patterns during summer lead to both ice cream consumption and swimming, which leads to an increased chance of drowning and shark attacks, or summer means more gatherings in which conflicts may arise, resulting in homicides…the two correlated increases are linked as causation.

The same challenge is seen when a veteran commits a crime, or breaks down, or acts in some socially unacceptable way…their military service MUST have been a causal factor in the crime.

In the summer of 2008, I had a Solider in my platoon that experienced a mental breakdown, which led to us referring him to a local inpatient facility for a period of time. Myself and the Soldier's squad leader took him to the facility, wanting to make sure he was all right. The Soldier was a young enlisted person, relatively lower-ranking and had only been in the service for a couple of years. He had deployed once, for a short period of time, during which he saw no active combat or was exposed to any traumatic events. By all accounts of those who had served with him, the deployment was as "uneventful" as any deployment could have been.

When we arrived at the facility, as the Soldier was filling out the intake paperwork, the intake coordinator asked, "have you ever been deployed" and when he answered, "yes", she started writing down a paragraph of information without asking any further questions! The reality was, this Soldier had mental health concerns from BEFORE he joined the military. Certainly, some experiences in the military may have exacerbated these challenges, but this young man had been in and out of foster care and had a challenging relationship with his adoptive parents…each of which were a factor in the situation that led to his breakdown, NOT his military deployment.

Another challenge, in this particular instance, is assuming that this veteran received some type of specialized formal training in the military that "turned him into" a "killing machine." This veteran in Dallas was a Carpentry and Masonry Specialist in the Army Reserves…hardly a highly-trained Special Operations soldier, or even an advanced marksman like members of the U.S. Army Marksmanship Unit[3]. The fact that he deployed to Afghanistan like millions of other veterans has less to do with what happened on that day in Dallas than what was going on with him personally. It would be professionally unethical of me to conduct an analysis of this individual; he and I never met, and I am not trained in or specialize in personality assessment of public figures. For me to speculate on what his motives, reasons, or drives were, as a mental health professional, could be construed as expert opinion that should be taken as fact. Nothing could be farther from the truth…where my opinion does come into play, however, is through an understanding of human nature and the military mindset.

Labeling anyone as any particular thing is counterproductive to getting to the true understanding of the situation. There are very real issues that need to be addressed by our society, and creating division only leads to more division. To understand and change, we must listen for wisdom rather than a lack of knowledge, we must narrow the gaps and distances between each other, and we must raise and address the core issues that face us rather than getting distracted by the rhetoric and venom.

Veterans, the military didn't just teach you to shoot straight and march far. It taught you how to solve problems, persevere in the face of overwhelming obstacles against you, and to be strong in order to prevent violence. Let's try to use that to help each other and our communities.

V IS FOR VETERAN, NOT VILLAIN, VICTIM, OR VINDICATOR

Over a period of two weeks in 2016, former service members committed heinous and horrifying attacks on American soil[1]. Are these the only crimes that have been committed in those two weeks? Of course not. They are not even the only crimes that have been committed by veterans in those two weeks.

This is not a political article, because I don't write those. Not my area of expertise. This is not a commentary on race in America, because there are enough of those going around, some good, some inflammatory. Whose side am I on? My father was a police officer and my brother-in-law and nephew are black. You better believe that all three of their lives matter to me and everyone in my family. I'm not choosing sides on this one, because I'm on humanity's side.

No, this is going in another direction, one that I touched on previously about how a veteran's military service does not automatically turn them into a killing machine, any more than a LEO's profession or a person's ethnicity turns them into a killing machine. There is a tendency to identify a veteran as one of three archetypes, mostly in the media, but sometimes in the veteran's community.

After the first incident, I had a good conversation with a fellow veteran, Casey Schoettmer. Casey works as an Employment and Training Specialist for qualifying veterans. As a military retiree, he certainly has a vested interest in the way that veterans are viewed, because that describes how he is viewed. Casey said something to me:

"The media really does a strange thing when it portrays us. I say that we're only portrayed as three things: Villain, Victim, or Vindicator."

Let that sink in for a minute. Five, eight, fifteen, or twenty-plus years of service, boiled down into three labels. Not father, or daughter, or radical, if that's what fits. No, just three neat categories that a veteran should fit into. What has been seen in the news lately is the veteran as a Villain. I receive daily updates on news stories that are connected to veteran mental health; just this morning, there was an article about how police shootings draw attention to Veterans' Mental Health[2], another highlighting the fact that both shooters were veterans[3], a look at the mind of the Baton Rouge shooter[4], and another about police shootings and American Veterans' mental health[5]. This is nothing new, of course, the focus is on current events, but Charles Whitman[6] and John Allen Muhammad[7] were both in the military. I was not around when killed 16 people at the University of Texas, but I recall the events around the DC Sniper shooting in 2002. While

Muhammad's service was mentioned, it was not highlighted as a cause or impetus for his rampage.

Another of the categories, roundly rejected by many veterans, is the idea of the veteran as a Victim. Because they deployed to combat, they are somehow broken or damaged in some way. I experienced this a couple of months ago; at a weekend retreat that had attendees from a bunch of different backgrounds, one gentlemen said, "I was really looking forward to this weekend, hanging out with a bunch of veterans. Helping others is what I do…I have always wanted to help out the stray dog or the broken winged bird." This is more closely aligned with how the social services or helping community sees veterans: fragile individuals that must be coddled and protected. And veterans often feed into this themselves; Casey described another scenario in which a veteran was told that he couldn't raise chickens, possibly because it violated some type of community law or ordinance. The individual thought that he should be allowed to do it solely on the basis that he was a veteran. There are times when veterans buy into a sense of entitlement, that they are entitled to get what they want on the basis of their veteran status. I don't know about you, but I only want what I was promised, and nowhere in my enlistment contract did it say that I would be able to raise a flagpole in my yard if my community laws prohibit it.

Strangely enough, the third label, Vindicator, or hero, is also rejected by many veterans I talk to. Lieutenant Colonel Charles Kettles received the Congressional Medal of Honor, decades after braving a hot LZ in order to extract 40 members of the 101st. In one article[8], Lt. Col. Kettles is said to have "focused on the other men involved in the rescue and said, 'The only thing that really matters' are the lives that were saved." Look through the media accounts of those veterans, current and former, who received the Medal of Honor, and you'll see a theme…it wasn't about me, it was about my brothers. I'm not a hero, they were. I've talked about it before in other posts, most veterans reject the Vindicator label as much as they reject the Victim or Villain label.

Why is this? Because we're just us. We're screwed up, strong, goofy humans who defy description because we're a bunch of individuals. We are not what we are labeled as, and we are not even what we seem to be sometimes. When I talk to veterans who are twisted up in their gut because of something they did or something they failed to do while deployed to combat, I suggest to them that they reject the label. We are not our actions; we are not monsters, although some have done some monstrous things. We are not heroes, although we may have done some heroic things.

What we are, is human. For me, American. The only V that I want to be labeled with, the only V that I accept, is the V that stands for Veteran.

THE STRIPES TELL A STORY...BUT NOT THE WHOLE STORY

On the Army Dress Uniform, there are a series of hash marks on one sleeve that indicate how long the Soldier has been in the service, and hash marks on the other sleeve that indicates how long the Soldier served overseas in a combat zone. The Army, in it's never-ending quest to be euphemistic, call these hash marks "overseas service bars."[1] Veterans, in their never-ending quest to call it like it is with no BS, call them "combat stripes."

Recently, I had the pleasure of spending some time with an old Army buddy, one of the Section Sergeants that served with me when I was a Platoon Sergeant in Afghanistan. He works far from the mountains of Afghanistan now, somewhere in the vast military-governmental complex that is Washington, D. C. He was telling me of an experience when he had the occasion to wear his dress uniform to work one day. He works in a multi-service location that includes many civilian workers, and some of them asked him "what all those stripes meant." He explained to them the difference between the service stripes and the combat stripes, but then he said he told them something that struck me: it's not the number of combat stripes that count, but the spaces between them.

You see, each combat stripe represents six months of overseas service. For each of the services, the tours are different lengths, and even within the services tour lengths vary based on the military specialty. In general, Army combat tours were twelve months long in the beginning of Iraq and Afghanistan, fifteen months between 2007 and 2009, and nine months later in the conflicts. Therefore, if a veteran participated in one 15 month tour, one 12 month tour, and one 9 month tour, then those three years of combat service would be represented by six combat stripes. That's a lot of stuff to be represented by six bits of cloth.

The thing is, as my friend so insightfully pointed out, the space between those stripes wasn't a cakewalk, either. The time between combat tours, especially during the height of the conflicts, was taken up by an immense amount of time away from the family. Field Training Exercises, trips to the National Training Center[2], trips to the Joint Readiness Training Center[3], temporary duty assignments, schools, any number of things that needed to happen to help the Soldier prepare for the next deployment while also maintaining career progression.

In some sense, the combat time is easy; we know where everything is, whether on a huge base or our small outpost. We know when the chow hall opens, we know the best latrine to go to; after learning the routine, we are pretty familiar with it. There are thousands of service members deployed with us, each responsible for their own job. I didn't have to gather my own intelligence on the routes we were using to provide security escort, I didn't have to make sure the generator was working properly to supply power to our command center. Not to oversimplify or diminish the danger that was often present, but my platoon and I had a job to do and the others around us had a job that they did, and we trusted it to happen.

Fast forward to the space between those stripes. All of a sudden, we are back in the "real world," dealing with chaotic and unpredictable lives. Those of us who were married: grocery shopping, parent teacher conferences, paying the bills. Those of us who were not married: avoiding the details that always seemed to be given to the Single Soldiers, perhaps looking for someone who would be willing to go grocery shopping with us, and create the opportunity for future parent teacher conferences. On top of this whipsaw of obligations is the memory of what happened during the last combat stripe, and knowing that the next combat stripe is not that far away.

The space between the stripes is significant for the families, not just for the spouses and children but for the parents of the service members as well. The space is filled with joy, and uncertainty, and confusion. Deployments change service members. It's not always bad change, and it's certainly not always good change, but it is change from what was before. That takes some adjustment, and so the family who is also getting used to the idea that the last stripe has been completed is getting used to the idea that the next one is coming up pretty quick.

Consider the space before and after the stripes. You can pack a lot of growing up in the stripes between those two spaces, a lifetime of experience that was significant and often challenging. Even if we weren't six or eight or ten years older than the person we were before we started earning them, the experiences impacted us in such a way that we change. Anyone can recognize that they are not the same person as their eighteen-year-old self…add experience in combat to that mix, and you increase that change exponentially.

If you're not a veteran, but know of some, take some time on Memorial Day to hear their stories. Maybe they don't want to talk about it…if that's the case, they'll let you know. If you have a veteran in your life who you know served overseas, it's likely that they lost someone in combat, and that is a burden that lingers between the stripes and carries on long after the last stripe has been sewn.

For veterans, take this time to remember your fallen brothers and sisters. Remember their lives, as messy and complicated and hilarious as they were, just as you remember their sacrifice. If the end is the only thing that is in focus, you are robbing yourself of the pleasure of remembering the good times, just as you are robbing your brother and sister of the true celebration of their life. I believe that I owe it to those who sacrificed to live well, rather than to fade away living a dysfunctional existence, and all veterans have the ability to make the choice of which one we decide to do.

What stories do the spaces between your stripes tell? Share them with others, so that they will be able to honor the service and sacrifice that those spaces, and the stripes, represent.

OZ, THE GREAT AND POWERFUL

One of the things that I've noticed when working with veterans, and something I've experienced myself, is the tendency to feel like we're about to be discovered as a fraud or a phony. It's like we're the Great Oz[1], building this image (or brand, if you will) of competent, professional businesspeople; but really, we're just a regular old schmuck behind the curtain.

I think much of it has to do with the transition from a military mindset to a civilian mindset. My personal experience is that the military is a very self-contained world; it is divided into "on-post" and "off-post", in which our daily lives in the military are the "real" world, and anything outside the gates was something that we did to get what we needed: entertainment, food, housing even. Even our off-post residence tends to be clustered with others who live on base; in my neighborhood, everyone within five houses of me are either current, former, or retired military.

We are so focused on the mission and the daily requirements of our duties, that we sometimes forget that there is real stuff happening. When I was in the Army, I had no clue where the bus station was, was not aware of any veteran-specific homeless prevention programs, or could find the local soup kitchen on a map. It's not that we lived in a sheltered la-la-land or that what I was doing had any more or less significance than the societal challenges outside; we were so focused on doing what we needed to do that we didn't have time to consider these things.

It's as if I lived with my back to the fence of my military base, focusing on my mission. It was absolutely right and necessary that I did so, because I had a job to do. Upon transition, it's like an entirely different world opened up, one that played by rules that I was not aware of and whose language I didn't know. It was if I was blown into an entirely different world by a runaway hot air balloon, like Oz, and had to figure out how best to fit in.

So I focused on deliberately learning the new rules of the professional world. Socks match your pants, not your shoes; who knew? You mean I shouldn't wear a brown belt with black shoes? Why not? Collared shirts, business cards, watches. Profanity, or a deliberate lack of it. It was strange, and just didn't feel right. After spending over twenty years in one mindset, I had to shift to an entirely different one, and it was like trying to adjust from one climate to another.

Other veterans I talk to echo the same thing, in private. "I just don't feel like I fit in." A friend who works for an outstanding veteran support organization told me, "what we're doing is so important, a guy like me shouldn't be anywhere near it!" It's not that we sell ourselves short, although that is a part of it. Veterans were capable professionals in their military careers, responsible for hundreds or millions of dollars worth of equipment, and more importantly, the safety of those we had responsibility for. We were used to that, though; we grew up in it, mostly, and had it modeled for us with good or bad examples from the leaders that came before us. These were living, breathing individuals that we saw all the time, not people who populated the self-help books, TED talks, or motivational blogs. Our professional self-development consisted of those things that made us better leaders, or better warriors, not better business people.

So the old carnival con man lands in Oz. He has to figure out a way to survive, and the way he arrived, people just assumes he's a wizard; he arrived like a wizard, says things that are what people would assume a wizard would say, and does wizardy things. It's a classic example of perception creating reality...if it walks like a duck and quacks like a duck, people are going to start treating it like a duck. Deep inside, though, there are questions; the carny knows that he can't keep up the charade forever, so he is more anxious, more uncertain, and builds up the façade even more.

No, I'm not calling veterans fakes or phonies. It's just that we sometimes feel that way. We keep thinking that someone is going to walk into their office and say, "Ha! Caught you! I know you're just a grunt at heart! What are you doing here?" I've talked to mentors in the mental health counseling field who are extremely successful, that I respect absolutely, and have been working in the industry for decades...and they feel the same way.

I remember when I was promoted from Specialist to Sergeant. I was walking along the sidewalk to the military clothing store, and I sneezed; a lower-ranking Soldier walking the opposite way stopped and said, "Bless You, Sergeant." I paused for a minute...who was he talking to? Oh, right, me. I had the same experience later in my career, after being promoted to Sergeant First Class; two other NCOs came up to ask me a question and stood at Parade Rest. I had to look behind me to see if there was a Sergeant Major standing there! I can imagine the old circus guy reacting the same way when the people of Oz started treating him like a wizard: "um, are you talking to me?"

The thing is, the wizard actually did solve the problems that Dorothy and her crew laid before him. He was as much of a wizard that was needed when the time came. Although we may feel like imposters, the innate problem solving ability of veterans, the values that we learned, the skills that we developed, means that we are exactly the kind of people needed where we are.

Maybe we need to start paying attention to the veteran behind the curtain, because they're gonna get things done.

ZERO TO SIXTY IS FUN, SIXTY TO ZERO NOT SO MUCH

Have you ever experienced the rush of thrill that comes from rapid acceleration? There's something about going from zero to sixty in less than eight seconds that brings a smile to my face. Hundreds of experiences attempt to capitalize on our human desire for rapid acceleration: roller coasters, skydiving, motorcycles. While there is certainly a factor of a sense of danger, there is also the pure joy in speed. While I enjoy endurance events in the Olympics, there's something exciting about watching Usain Bolt run 100 meters in less than 10 seconds.

If I hope we can all agree that going from zero to sixty is a heck of a lot of fun, can we also agree that going from sixty to zero is just as much not fun?

Rapid deceleration is nowhere near as fun as rapid acceleration. There are physics involved, of course, but often it's just downright painful. The four to six seconds after jumping out of the airplane (for paratroopers, that is) is inevitably followed by the opening shock of the canopy, which can be seriously painful if you're not prepared for it.

I hear veterans who often feel as though leaving the military service was like going from sixty to zero in no time at all.

Veterans leave the military like snow falls from the clouds. According to an article from 2014[1], over 250,000 veterans are expected to leave the service every year over the next five years. Just like that snowstorm, however, each individual service member's experience on leaving the service is unique and different. These 250k veterans will retire, complete their term of service, be administratively discharged, medically separated, or countless combinations of any of these. Some, like myself, have a long time to plan; I was considering the right time for my retirement a full three years before I chose to leave. I had a solid idea about what was going to happen eighteen months before my actual retirement date, and I was blessed to be able to have that opportunity. Not all veterans are as lucky as me, however, and it would be inaccurate to say that there wasn't some level of hesitation or trepidation on my part.

As I've written elsewhere, a veteran's time in the military can bring about a significant source of pride, purpose and meaning. There are certainly times of frustration and boredom, but overall, there is a sense of belonging and accomplishment that goes along with service in the military that is often difficult for veterans to explain, and just as equally difficult to replicate. When a veteran leaves the service, there can certainly be a sense that their lives have rapidly decelerated to a point where it's just not that much fun.

We experience this when we return from an overseas deployment. It's as if we are driving at (or above) speed on a four-lane highway, while life back home is driving at the speed of the access road. Veterans have to merge their rapid-paced accelerated life to the comparatively slow and steady lives of their family and friends. This merge takes a lot of awareness on both sides, which often doesn't happen.

The challenge is when a veteran can't recognize the change, and doesn't really want the change to happen. If a veteran is medically discharged, they're not ready to get out. They quite possibly had hopes and dreams that will now be unfulfilled. Personal goals, like promotion and leadership opportunities, or community goals, like being able to mentor the next generation of Soldiers or Marines. If they stay in contact with their old buddies, then they may see them continue to achieve those goals of promotion, and think, "man, that could have been me." These thoughts can lead to anger…at themselves, the military, whoever they find to blame for their discharge…or loss. Grief. Depression. The rapid deceleration, not having time to come to terms with the change, can amplify these feelings.

Another personal experience story. As part of our unit's changeover in Afghanistan, there was a requirement to help the other unit take over our mission. We tell them about what we do, they follow us around for a bit, half of our Soldiers and half of their Soldiers conduct the mission, then we follow them around for a bit, then they have the mission. As we were leaving, for whatever reason, our timeline was compressed, and we had one more mission to conduct. They took the lead on it, and me and one of my guys went along just as observers and advisors. Six hours after we returned from that three-day mission, we were on a plane leaving the country.

With an abrupt change like this, there is a tendency to question whether or not there were things left undone. There is something to be said about not having regrets, but when a veteran is doing something they love which is also extremely important, it's almost impossible not to have regrets.

One thing the military does is teach us how to be part of a team. None of us is as important as all of us. You know, intellectually, that you are just one small part of a million-person force, a snowflake in the storm, one star in the vast expanse of the universe. It's another thing, however, to have that knowledge shown to you in clear detail when the military continues to function well after you are no longer a part of it.

The thing about going from zero to sixty: it's a lot of fun, but it's not sustainable. At some point, you are going to have to slow down and stop. And going from sixty to zero: it's painful, and difficult, but wishing you could go back to the fast lane when it's no longer an option is an exercise in futility. You can learn from that experience, though, and heal, and move on. Going from sixty to zero may not be fun, but it's certainly educational.

VETERANS MAY NOT HAVE PICTURES, BUT THEY CERTAINLY HAVE MEMORIES

While I was in the military, I didn't take a whole lot of pictures. I never wanted to be a "combat tourist," knowing full well that I could be missing out on some really great memories later in life. Don't get me wrong, I love looking at pictures of time past, the "man, can you imagine how young we were then" or "Do you remember when the three of us went..."

I do wish that something had come over me in some specific moments, though, that I could have taken a picture at just the right time. There are some memories that I have where words simply do not do them justice. I recall one day at Forward Operating Base Bostick, a memory that I hope will last forever; our platoon had just escorted supplies to the base the night prior, and we were probably getting ready to leave again that night. Sometime in the afternoon, we heard someone outside our tent exclaim, "You have to come see this!" Of course, for veterans, that could have meant any number of things, from some weird wildlife to something cool about to happen with explosives, but not this time.

As I exited our tent, I look to the east and was frozen. There, above the mountains of the Hindu Kush, was the largest, most brilliant double rainbow I have ever seen. The two arcs stretch from mountaintop to mountaintop, vibrant and beautiful. I was amazed at such a striking sight over a combat zone, and full of thankfulness for the opportunity to be at that place, at that time, in order to be able to witness it.

I was also a moron for not taking a picture.

There are other memories, frozen in my mind, that I didn't know were a picture moment. I sometimes wish I could find one of those police sketch artists so I could describe my memory to them, and I could turn it into something tangible to show to people.

I remember the last time I saw Sergeant First Class Jason Fabrizi[1]. Jay and I weren't much more than acquaintances; we were deployed in different battalions of the same brigade in Iraq, and we ran into each other from time to time. During the deployment in Afghanistan, he was a Platoon Sergeant for a Cavalry Troop that provided overwatch for us as we escorted supplies to his base.

FOB Bostick, like many of the larger bases overseas, had an MWR building that housed games, a TV, pool tables and ping pong tables, and walls lined with books that had been donated for the troops. I always enjoyed looking at the books, browsing for some hidden surprise. There were two entrances to the room: one, which led to a small porch that overlooked the Kunar river and out to the showers, and another that led out to the rest of the camp. As I was looking over the books in the sunken area near the television, I hear someone come in the door by the porch: it was Jay, obviously coming from the shower. I can see him now, towel slung over his shoulder, on his way out the other door, on the other side of the pool table, a lopsided grin of recognition on his face. I don't remember the conversation we had…something like, "how's it been going, rough stuff out there, thanks for what you're doing" on both of our parts. Probably ended with something like, "I'll catch you later." I didn't. Less than two weeks later, he was gone.

I should have taken a picture.

I have two images in my mind's eye of Sergeant Eduvigues Wolf[2], the NCO we lost in October of that year. SGT Wolf and her husband, Josh, were deployed in separate units of the same battalion as well. One of the clearest memories I have is of a training exercise in Louisiana that we all participated in prior to the deployment. We were housed in a large tent, and I recall looking over and seeing Duvi and Josh huddled together on a cot, smiling and laughing about something they were looking at. Most likely, pictures of their daughters back home with the grandparents…but I remember them, heads together, the entire larger world forgotten and replaced by their own smaller world. As it should be.

I recall memories later in the deployment. SGT Wolf had spent some time in our company operations center, working as an Operations NCO for our First Sergeant and Commander. She was often the first person I saw when I came in to talk to the 1SG and CO, and the last person I saw when I left…always positive, usually smiling, the picture in my memory is of her sticking her head around the corner as I'm walking down the hallway.

I should have taken a picture.

I also have memories of the time and place when I found they were taken from us. I choose not to share them here, not because I want to avoid the memory or suppress it, but because I want to choose to celebrate their lives rather than focus on their deaths. Jay was a great leader to his Soldiers, and he trained them well. Duvi was a loving wife, devoted mother, and an outstanding NCO who could be depended upon.

For veterans, memories are both precious and painful. Memorial Day can be both bitter and sweet, and we many times forget that we can choose which of those to experience. Many of the veterans I work with tend to focus on the end of the story rather than the entire story, to focus on the loss rather than the life. We focus on the snapshot, the picture, the freezeframe at the end of the movie and can sometimes forget about the entire movie of their lives.

If you are a veteran and are struggling with the memories you have, you are not alone. While we need to ensure that we remember those that we have lost, it is of no benefit if we become lost ourselves. Reach out to someone so you can talk about what is bothering you, and it will start to bother you less.

If you know of a veteran who appears to be struggling, let them know that help is out there. Support them, try to understand, do what you can to help them through this. Help them connect with a mental health professional that can assist them in getting things back in order.

And take a picture.

FOUR LESSONS LEARNED FROM A LATRINE STALL IN IRAQ

On military deployments, the bathroom situation is usually interesting. It is not often that the bathroom (or "latrine" or "head" or several other euphemisms less acceptable in polite company) is actually in the same building or area that you sleep in.

In Iraq in 2006, my unit was stationed on a Forward Operating Base in Northeast Baghdad. We lived and worked in a two-story dormitory style building that was one of a series of three. In between our building and the one next to it was a latrine trailer and a shower trailer, one each for both male and female Soldiers. Think of a fifth-wheel mobile home, only filled with toilet stalls and showers. This arrangement was shared by several different units, probably about three to four hundred of us.

Another interesting fact about military service members: we get bored easily, and find strange and interesting ways to amuse ourselves. In regards to this particular latrine, one of the ways that our Soldiers found to amuse themselves was graffiti. Lots of it. So much graffiti that one could literally spend hours reading the musings and thoughts of combat veterans deployed to a faraway land. To be honest, much of it was funny, as graffiti written by combat veterans is likely to be. Lots of stuff about Chuck Norris.

A lot of it wasn't funny, though. It started to get to the point where the graffiti in the male latrine started causing tension between people, the anonymity afforded by the bathroom wall bringing out the worst them, just like the anonymity and lack of face-to-face feedback sometimes brings out the worst in people on social media. So I decided to do something about it.

First, get rid of the graffiti. This was one of the first challenges, and why it got out of control; the command thought, "Well, if we clean it off, it will just come back, so there's no point." Lesson one: if you think there's no point in doing something, then there's no point in doing something. Don't accept a problem because you don't think there's a solution. Figure it out. So I made sure we could get it gone, and one of my subordinates spent a night scrubbing the walls. He said he enjoyed it, called it "meditative." Just goes to show you how boring things can sometimes get while on deployment.

Second, keep the graffiti from coming back. On each stall, we posted the Soldier's Creed[1] and the NCO Creed[2], one on each side. Laminated them. On the back of the door, right at eye level, we put the following sign:

ONLY COWARDS HIDE BEHIND WORDS WRITTEN
ANONYMOUSLY ON WALLS.

IF YOU FEEL LIKE YOU NEED TO READ SOMETHING, LOOK TO YOUR LEFT AND YOUR RIGHT AND BE REMINDED OF THE PROFESSIONAL THAT YOU ARE.

IF YOU HAVE AN URGE TO WRITE SOMETHING ON THIS WALL, COME FIND SERGEANT FIRST CLASS FRANCE, BUILDING ####, ROOM NUMBER ##, AND TELL HIM ABOUT IT

This was honestly an attempt by me to use my position in my unit to influence behavior, and not be a coward by not putting something on the wall anonymously. Amazingly, to my surprise, it worked. Lesson number two: even if you have a harebrained scheme that has no chance of working, give it a shot. You never know.

This experience reminded me of the broken window theory[3], in that an abandoned building without broken windows will likely remain intact until someone breaks a window. There is something about taking that first action to break a window that will keep most in society from doing it. Once the first window is broken, however, there seems to be a taboo that is broken as well, and others find it easy to break more windows. That's how it got with our bathroom graffiti: once it was acceptable, and nothing was done about it, it became more acceptable. When it was removed, it was much easier to maintain; sure, sometimes the signs were torn off, and sometimes someone wrote on the wall again, but someone else always told us about it and it was taken care of quickly. Lesson number three: sometimes solving a problem means maintaining the solution, not walking away considering the problem done.

Interestingly enough, that wasn't the end of the story. Sometime later, I was walking back to my building and heard someone calling my name. This guy runs up to me, and I look at him, wondering if I knew him.

"Sergeant France, there you are!" he said. I looked at his name, his unit.

"Do I know you?" I said.

"I'm from the unit next door," referring to the unit that was in the other building, "and I've been looking for you."

"Okay, what's up?"

"My Battalion Commander's an @!#*(#$," he said. I waited for him to continue.

"And…"

"Nothing, that's it. He made me so mad the other day that I was going to go in and write it on the wall, then I saw your sign, and figured I'd tell you instead of writing it on the wall."

"Okay, is there anything you need me to do? Like, is there a problem that I need to get involved in, like reporting it to someone or something?"

"Not really, it's just the Army," he said, then waved at me and walked down the street.

Now, I get it, this was just a young sergeant being a smartass. A goofy kid poking the bear a little bit, trying to break up the monotony of life while blowing off a little steam. That got me to thinking, though; why can't there be more of that? Organizations have their own internal investigative units that make sure that policies are being adhered to, but what if different organizations teamed up to allow people to blow off steam? I mean, it didn't matter to ME that he thought his Battalion Commander was a jerk. I was pretty well satisfied with mine. It's as if the guy that delivers sandwiches to our office now would come in and say, "Man, I really hate working for Jimmy Johns. I just don't like being so fast all the time." No sweat off my back, just takes a bit of my time and lets him blow off some steam. Lesson number four: always be flexible enough to respond to unintended reactions to your solution. You may find benefits that you didn't expect.

FOUR AREAS IN A VETERAN'S LIFE THAT REQUIRE BALANCE, AND HOW TO ACHIEVE IT

Have you ever been through rollover training while you were in the military, or worse, actually experienced a rollover[1]? A total loss of control, the vehicle that you're in reaches a tipping point and over it goes. Finding balance in our lives after leaving the service is one of the most important things we can do to ensure our future success. There are many things we need to balance...work and play, family and career, what we want to do and what we need to do. Before we can create equilibrium in those things however, it would be best if we could find balance within ourselves.

I've talked about the continuum between functional and dysfunctional. I deliberately chose to refrain from focusing on wellness vs. illness, out of a desire not to pathologize our experiences in the military. However, wellness is certainly a goal to be aspired to, for us to be as well as we could possibly be. The balance I am talking about here is the balance that leads to wellness.

In order to succeed in our transition out of the service, or out of combat, we must strive to maintain wellness in four different areas of our life: physical, mental, emotional, and spiritual.

If any one of these four areas is deficient, then we are not operating at our full potential. We are not as well, or as balanced, as we could be, and this could lead to more difficulties down the road.

Regarding physical wellness, this is something that many veterans do well...but how often do we maintain those habits after we leave the service? Outside of that, how many times did we ignore problems while were in the service, that came back to haunt us later? Veterans are often required to push themselves to their physical limits and beyond, and proudly do so. Do we sometimes do that to our detriment? Did jumping out of airplanes thirty-five too many times do as much harm as it did good? I wouldn't change any of them, of course, and if I could go back in time, I would probably increase the amount of jumps rather than decrease, but they certainly took a toll on my physical wellness. How about habits after we get out? Drinking too much, eating too much, exercising too little? Physical wellness is certainly something to pay attention to.

Often, when I talk to veterans about Mental and Emotional wellness, there is a misconception that I'm talking about the same thing. They are certainly intertwined, but they are separate and distinct. When I talk about mental wellness, I'm talking about your thoughts, your internal point of view, whether you see things positively or negatively. How you explain the world around you has a huge impact on how you get things done. I'm not talking about some Pollyana, pie-in-the-sky blind optimism, because let's be real, we always focused on the most likely course of action and the most dangerous course of action when planning something. Whether it was a range or a patrol, we always considered what could go catastrophically wrong. Planning for the worst case scenario is ingrained in the military mindset…it's why we always had three AT4s, a few Claymores, and a bunch of Frag grenades with us when we went out. Do we always need to be locked into that mindset, however? Constantly considering the worst case scenario keeps us trapped in a catastrophic mindset. I hear you saying to yourself, "that's great, but thinking positively about the future don't put food on the table." Absolutely. It's not always easy, and it's not always fun. You know what else wasn't always easy or fun? Basic training. You made it through that, didn't you?

As I mentioned, Emotional Wellness is closely tied to Mental Wellness, so much so that the two can impact each other like one wave impacts another. How many times in your service did you have a leader who was tactically sharp as a tack, who could slice through a problem like a knife through butter…but would fly off the handle at the seemingly smallest detail? We referred to those leaders as "bipolar" or "schizo" (and we can have an entirely different discussion about using serious mental conditions in such an off-hand way, but the reality is what it is. Doesn't make it right.) You may be on the right track professionally, doing all of the right things, connecting with all of the right people, but if you are overwhelmed emotionally, then you simply will not be as effective as you could possibly be. Your thinking may be on the right track, but if stress causes you to explode into anger or spiral into depression, then transition will be challenging. Alternatively, if you have too LITTLE emotion, then that can throw you off balance as well…distancing yourself emotionally from those around you, and from society, can bring it's own challenges.

Spiritual Wellness is something that is critical as well. I am not specifically talking about a particular religion, although that can certainly be a part of it. Being connected to something "other", feeling part of something larger and more important than yourself, can give you both meaning and purpose in your life. For me, personally, I don't believe that I would be able to help veterans in the way that I do if it were not for my faith in God and His Son. I find strength in my faith, in my spirituality, when I often do not have strength physically, mentally, or emotionally. Spiritual wellness also speaks to finding meaning and purpose in your life; many veterans struggle with a loss of a sense of meaning and purpose after they leave the service. Those that we interact with don't seem to understand what we went through, and worse, don't seem to want to understand. The need to find purpose and meaning in our lives is so significant that I will be devoting future posts to this point. I have talked to many veterans who have found their balance physically, become more aware of their thoughts and in control of their emotions, but still felt "empty inside" and unable to find any meaning in their lives or what they are doing.

Balancing physical, mental, emotional, and spiritual wellness can keep you from being injured in a catastrophic life rollover. If you are struggling in any of these areas, find someone to help. Reach out to a buddy, a counselor, a mentor, an advisor. You don't have to go through this transition alone, and no one…least of all me…wants to see another veteran succumb to a catastrophic life event.

FOR VETERANS, SOME THINGS CAN BE HARD TO LET GO

"In the end these things matter most: How well did you love? How fully did you live? How deeply did you let go?" — *Gautama Buddha*

I heard a story on the news about a group of four marines who took a picture on a beach in May of 1966, and recreated it 50 years later[1]. That, and a chance remark to a former soldier of mine, who happened to repeat it to a group of us on Facebook, got me thinking: some things can be hard to let go.

It can be hard for veterans to let go of our memories of the service. Sometimes, we take it too far, of course; a recent discussion warned against the trap of getting too caught up in our military experiences and missing out on life after the service. It can be hard to let go of the idea that "the good old days were always good" as the Billy Joel song goes, even though we know that the good old days had some pretty bad moments in them.

Without awareness, it can be hard to let go of the support that we received in the service. We always knew that, whatever base we went to, there was going to be a dining facility. We may never eat there, but we know that it's always there if we need it. HR will always be there in the form of post finance or the personnel section in our Battalion. If the internet goes out, go get someone from Commo or put in a request to the S6; when we come in the building in the morning, the light comes on when we hit the switch. In all of my years in the Army, I never had to worry about paying the electricity bill, even when I was a company First Sergeant. The water was always on, except when it wasn't, and it usually came back on pretty quick without much effort on my part. When we get out of the military, though, especially if we open our own business, a lot of those things that we never prepared ourselves for are front and center…and not letting go of the idea that I can stick my head out of my office and ask (or tell) someone to do something can certainly create challenges in our civilian lives.

It can be hard to let go of regrets that we had; regrets that we didn't choose that MOS[1] (or regrets that we chose the one we did), sometimes regrets that we did too much and regrets that we didn't do enough. Regrets that we didn't go to combat, and regrets that we did go to combat. If we get caught up in the "coulda, woulda, shoulda" thoughts about things that we didn't accomplish or the things that did happen that we weren't proud of, then we can get stuck in the past without looking forward to the future.

Sometimes, there are things that we don't want to let go of. I lost a friend of mine in a car accident on the night before Thanksgiving, 1994; at his memorial service they played "Wish You Were Here" by Pink Floyd during a memorial photo montage. Every time I hear that song on the radio, Joe

Parks comes to mind. The passage of time makes the pain of loss less, but it doesn't take it away entirely. The memory of Joe is certainly something that I don't want to let go of, and it has happened so often over the last twenty years that I don't think I will ever let go.

Sometimes the things that are hard to let go of are habits. Big habits, like the need to scan the room or the rooftops in order to feel safe; or small habits, like keeping all of your pocket stuff…keys, wallet, whatever…in one place so you can grab it and go the next morning. A couple of my habits that are hard to let go of revolve around coffee: in Afghanistan, my LT, section sergeants and I all shared a tent. We had a common coffeepot, and the first one up in the morning would fill the tank with bottled water and dump a scoop of fresh grounds on top of yesterday's old grounds and run it through…the presence of the coffee was what was important, not the quality. When I got back home, however, and did the same thing, my (long-suffering and very patient) wife looked at me like I was crazy. Now that we have one of those fancy pod-coffee things, I'll do the same…run three or four cups through the same grounds. It doesn't disrupt my life and it's something I picked up along the way…no real reason to let it go, so it hangs around.

"The chains of habit are too weak to be felt until they are too strong to be broken." — *Samuel Johnson*

The problem with not letting things go is when the things we don't let go start to get in the way of our progress in life. A friend of mine in Pittsburgh said that he often interviews veterans who are so fresh from combat that they are still shouting…if we don't let go of those combat habits, life is going to be just a bit more difficult. The key is becoming aware of the fact that we are going to have to change, and as I mentioned in a previous post, huge change is difficult.

If you are not a veteran, but someone who supports a veteran, and you're reading this, then great. Anything that can be done to help you understand veterans is outstanding. I'm not saying that the veteran you're interacting with can't explain it to you, but if they're struggling, then it is unlikely that they will do so…a remnant of another thing that is hard to let go of, the idea that we can and do get things done on our own.

If you're a veteran, and you're reading this, what kind of things are you not letting go? Is that okay with you, and not getting in the way of life? You don't have to change beyond what you feel comfortable with, but the ultimate benefit of change is personal growth. I don't ever want to let go of the ideals and experience that I gained in the military, while also knowing that I do need to let go of those things that get in the way now.

AM I DOING THIS WRONG? A VETERAN'S QUESTION

Maybe my point of view is somewhat skewed. I work with veterans daily who are struggling with challenges they are having as a result of their experiences. Relationships, reaction to both combat and non-combat trauma, lack of a sense of purpose and meaning, substance addiction. A lack of understanding about why they think the way they think, even sometimes a lack of awareness of the impact of how they're thinking has on their behavior.

Call them weak? You'll have me to deal with. The stress and pressure, which many who have not served or have not stood alongside those who have served are simply unaware of, is unfathomable. The appreciation that veterans have for the freedoms and luxuries that others take for granted is almost cliché.

At 19 years old, I slept on a cot for a year while deployed to Bosnia. My room in Kabul, considered a palace by many because I didn't have to share it with someone else, was a six foot by ten foot room that would be more properly described as a large closet. The sheer number…and weirdness…of things that were missed or gone without during a veteran's service is so long that your eyes would glaze over before you even got a quarter of the way through it. The strangest thing for me? Slurpees. After two tours in Germany, Iraq, Afghanistan (twice), North Africa, I miss me a Slurpee. I'll drink a Slurpee in the middle of a snowstorm, I don't care. Icees don't cut it…you know what I'm talking about…it has to be a Slurpee.

The sacrifice extends to our families. My children attended more different elementary schools than most kids attended in their lifetime. It's not urban legend that military families move often; my wife and I lived in nine different houses in the first ten years of our marriage. Contrary to what many civilians experience, we have dozens of different "jobs," often at the same time, many at different times throughout our time in the military.

Don't get me wrong, this isn't a "my life sucks more than yours, so cut me some slack or give me some good stuff" post. It's not a "be appreciative for what you have, because others ain't got it so good, either" post.

No, this is a post about a question that I think a lot of veterans have:

What if I'm doing this wrong?

The "if" could be dozens of different things. This relationship. Job hunting. My way of dealing with what I saw in combat. Transition out of the military, whether it's after four years or twenty-four. For some veterans, those most hurting and vulnerable, may even ask if they are doing Life wrong, and come to a heartbreaking and unbearable conclusion.

Maybe this is a dark and depressing post to be sharing. Like I said, maybe my point of view of veterans is skewed, but with the insanely and tragically high rate of veteran suicide, the stress that military life puts on families, the gulf between what veterans experienced and those who are not veterans or family members don't understand, I think that this doubt in someone who was so previously confident is important to recognize.

What if I'm doing this wrong? When that doubt starts to creep in, maybe the veteran starts to lose hope. Maybe they start to wish for the Glory Days, as Springsteen said. What we…all of us, not just veterans…seem to forget is, like Billy Joel said, "the good old days weren't always good, and tomorrow ain't as bad as it seems."

Do we, as a community, really want that? Do we want those who have volunteered to serve our country to question whether or not their service was worth it, only to get out and find that it is a challenge for them to get health care, stay housed, to find meaning and purpose in their lives?

In his book, Tribe[1], Sebastian Junger writes: "Humans are so strongly wired to help one another – and enjoy such enormous social benefits from doing so – that people regularly risk their lives for complete strangers." Upon reading that, my question was: what happens when your will to help others no longer results in social benefits? No, this generation of veterans is not receiving the scorn or indifference that previous generations have, but understanding is not also there.

On Veteran's Day, on Memorial Day, the 4th of July, any of the patriotic holidays, appreciate veterans, absolutely. Thank them for their service. But maybe do more than that…maybe listen to them. Don't judge them. Try to understand them. Appreciate them by allowing them to know that what sacrifices they made, what sacrifices their families made, are absolutely worth it.

Let them know that they're not doing this wrong at all.

EIGHT THINGS A VETERAN WANTS THEIR MENTAL HEALTH COUNSELOR TO KNOW

As a professional counselor and military veteran, one of the most rewarding aspects of the work that I do is helping other veterans come to a point of awareness and understanding about their experiences in the military, and setting the stage for change if that's what the veteran is willing to do. Here are eight different points that I believe veterans would like their mental health counselor to know before working with them.

1. I'm not sure this is necessary

There's something about sitting down and talking to a stranger that a veteran finds challenging. Whether it is the fact that the veteran is going to share their darkest, most intimate secrets with you, or the fact that they have tried to do the same with others before and have been betrayed or hurt, it's going to be difficult for a veteran to even reach out for help. I've heard it so many times that it's almost become standard language: "I'm not even sure why I'm here. I mean, I should be able to handle these things, right?" The military mindset of enduring hardship without complaint remains, even though the veteran is no longer in the service. It's important to help the veteran to understand the necessity of processing the events they experienced.

2. I'm really, really trusting you

Trust is a huge thing for veterans, as it is for many clients. From the moment that a service member joins the military, though, trust is a factor that is as critical as food and water for their emotional and sometimes physical survival. They trust their fellow service members to support them, to have their back, just as their brothers and sisters expect support. They trust in their leaders, their equipment, their training. Sometimes, that trust is betrayed, often in ways that the veteran doesn't really understand, and that creates conflicts with what they believe to be right and what they experience in the world. For a veteran to sit down with a mental health counselor is the ultimate trust fall, placing not just their own life in your hands but often some of the most precious and meaningful things they can think of…the memories of those they've trusted in the past.

3. The only reason I'm here is because I'm tired of feeling the way I do

In my experience, I've rarely known veterans to seek mental health treatment proactively. Instead, it's usually a matter of, "I realized I need to get help" or "I'm here because someone told me I needed to get help." There is an internal struggle between not wanting to admit to needing help and recognizing that it's necessary and important. As long as the need is not apparent, then the action will not be taken. Unfortunately, there is usually some challenge in their lives that has become more significant than the barriers to treatment that exist, both in their own mind and in their environment. The fact that the veteran has been able to overcome the challenges they face in asking for help is a huge indicator that they really need to be there.

4. I really want to be able to talk...

If there's one thing a veteran likes to do, it's tell stories, and they have a whole lot of them. Stories about what happened to them, stories they tell themselves about what has happened to them, stories all over the place. Many of them are funny as hell, a large portion of them are unbelievable, and many are some of the most difficult things to listen to that you'll ever experience. The veteran has a desire to be able to talk about their experiences and understand them.

5. ...but have no intention of doing so...

Simultaneously, however, the veteran has zero intention of telling the story they so desperately want people to hear. It might be because they feel like it's an exercise in futility, that no one who has not been in the military or been to combat can possibly understand what they experienced. It might be that they are afraid that if they dig up the past, they will be haunted by the memories even more than they already are. For whatever the reason, the veteran both wants people to understand, without having to tell them about it. Waiting patiently for one of those conditions to change is critical.

6. ...and will shut down if I feel like you're judging me.

A particular way to destroy any type of rapport with a veteran is to express horror, condemnation, or revulsion at their experiences. I recognize that a nonjudgmental point of view and unconditional positive regard are some of the most fundamental aspects of our counseling practice, but actually putting these into practice can be difficult when working with veterans. Seeing horror or judgment on someone else's face can be like the veteran is looking in the mirror; it validates what they feel about themselves.

7. I don't think that you'll be able to understand what I experienced

This is another theme that I've heard many times from veterans: "they don't get it, because they haven't been there." It's as if the counselor has no legitimacy when it comes to life experience, although the veteran appreciates the effort you must have gone through to get the education you have. It goes to a fundamental hope that the veteran has...that you will be able to help...that is also tied to an equally strong belief...that you will not be able to. Developing an understanding of veterans and military culture that goes beyond just learning acronyms and rank structure can go a long way to establishing legitimacy in the veteran's eyes. The idea of, "you should trust me because I'm a professional who can help" means much less to a veteran than, "I've taken the time to learn about you and what's important to you."

8. I have no desire to be coddled, revered, or bullied.

Three things that I have seen that a veteran finds challenging: being treated like a victim, being treated like a hero, or being treated like a child. They will reject the first, deny the second, and resist the third. I once heard another professional say, "I think that I could really work with veterans, because I'm very nurturing...I love rescuing broken-winged birds." Approaching the veteran from this point of view, that they are a damaged and fragile human that just needs to be cared for, is a sure way to get them to reject any assistance you may want to provide. It may be true that they're fragile and damaged, but they're not used to being treated that way. Similarly, treating the veteran like a hero is something they don't want. To many veterans, the most heroic people they know are the brothers and sisters that didn't make it back from combat, and comparing themselves to those true heroes is a challenge. Again, maybe it's true, maybe they had done some significantly heroic things, but they don't see it that way. And finally, being forceful with a veteran..."you should just get over it" or "I'll tell you what you need to do" is something that will increase resistance rather than reduce it.

EIGHT THINGS A MENTAL HEALTH PROFESSIONAL WANTS A VETERAN TO KNOW

A recent post listed eight things that a veteran wants their mental health counselor to know. It's extremely important that mental health professionals take the time to understand the cultural aspect of military service, and how the veteran's time in the military has impacted them. It's often one of the most critical barriers that veterans face when seeking mental health services: the need to explain themselves and their service to a provider that has little to no understanding about their experiences.

The list was written from my own experience as a combat veteran, and from what I've learned from veterans in my own work; this post is looking at things from the other side, based on my experiences as a mental health counselor.

There are some definite misconceptions about the mental health counseling profession that is perpetuated by stigma, both from peers and the community as well as from veterans themselves. We don't want to be seen as "weak" or "damaged," although seeking help is not weakness, and if you had a broken foot, you'd go to see a doctor without thinking you're damaged. Perhaps these thoughts will help overcome some of those misconceptions.

1. This isn't about Freud on the couch.

One of the most common misconceptions about mental health counseling is that you are going to lie on a couch and talk about your mother. We may, in fact, talk about your mother, but only if that's something that is causing you concern. Freudian psychoanalysis is only one therapeutic discipline, and it's unlikely that you will experience it when you reach out.

2. This stuff actually works.

There is actually an extremely good chance that working with a mental health professional will resolve some of the challenges you're experiencing with anxiety, depression, anger, relational issues, just about anything. There is no need to continue to suffer if someone who knows what they're talking about can help to relieve that suffering. Most therapeutic modalities provided by competent professionals are effective those misconceptions.

3. You're going to have to talk about what's bothering you...

Yes, at some point, you will have to talk about whatever is causing you to reach out and seek help. There are some therapeutic styles that don't require this at all, and there are some that require a lot of it. The thing is, it's not going to have to happen right away. I often meet with veterans who, on the first day that we meet, they want to tell me about the worst day of their lives. Take it slow, learn some techniques with how to cope with the emotions and reactions that recalling and retelling those events will bring about, and most importantly, learn to trust your counselor. Then, when you're ready, we can talk about those events.

4.   ...and it's not as bad as you think it's going to be.

How much worse could it be than the nightmares, the intrusive memories, the constant hypervigilance that's keeping you on edge all the time? "It's actually helpful to talk about it" is something I've heard often. It's as if these thoughts are trapped in your head, with nowhere to go, so they just keep bouncing around gaining speed and mass until they shred everything inside. By getting it out of our head, talking about it, we can examine the validity of those memories and our attitudes towards them. If we avoid seeking help for the broken foot because the fear of the pain of surgery is too much, then we will have to live with the pain of the unbroken and poorly healed foot.

5.   It's not all about pills and meds.

There are some mental health conditions that absolutely do require medication. There are also some benefits to medication to control mood and emotion, especially when first starting to seek treatment. Consider them as training wheels, though; they are there to help stabilize the bike until you can learn to stabilize the bike on your own. There are differences between psychiatrists, psychologists, and mental health counselors. Psychiatrists prescribe medications, psychologists and counselors do not. Learning how to cope with these experiences without medication can help reduce your reliance upon them.

6.   I actually know what I'm talking about.

I didn't get this degree out of the bottom of a Crackerjack box. Licensed mental health professionals have to have, at a minimum, a Master's Degree from an accredited program at an actual college or university. In order to obtain, or to be working towards, licensure in the state that I'm operating in, I have to meet some very specific criteria for education, experience, and examination. Just like a Doctor or Lawyer, I wouldn't be able to do this job if I weren't qualified. More importantly, I understand the history, theoretical basis, and techniques of my profession. I adhere to a professional code of ethics, and I am a member of professional organizations that help me to maintain my understanding of my profession. If you trust nothing else about me from the beginning, trust that I have the training and experience to help you get to where you want to go.

7.   I'm not going to give you advice or tell you what to do.

This isn't Dr. Phil or Dear Abby. Chances are, you've got enough people in your life telling what you should or shouldn't do, but that's not what I'm here for. I often tell veterans I work with, "I'm not an answering machine, I'm more of a mirror." I can ask questions, make statements, help you to understand how your experiences impacted you. I can help you become more aware of why things are the way they are and how they affect you today, but I'm not going to tell you what you should or shouldn't do. You do that enough to yourself. Together, we can examine how you think and what you believe, and you may be able to come to a greater understanding that you don't want to think or believe things in a certain way anymore, but I won't tell you what to do. If that's what you're looking for..."just tell me how to stop feeling this way and I'll do it"...then there's another misconception we can work on when you come to see me.

8.   If you and I don't click, then let me help you find someone you do click with.

One of the challenges is that, when you were in the military, you only saw your assigned provider. If you and your doc didn't get along, tough, that's the only one you got. It doesn't have to be that way once you get out; not everyone works the same way. I've had veterans that started to work with me that didn't really connect with the whole military-NCO-turned-counselor thing. I'm a big guy and was obviously a Senior NCO when I was in the military; some veterans have real problems with that, as their experiences in the military were around not trusting guys and gals like me. Not a problem...let me find someone who you can connect with. I'm a professional that keeps things professional, and if I take the fact that we don't have a connection personally, then I'm not keeping things professional. It's about you, not about me as the counselor; it's about your needs, not mine.

THE MOMENT I REALIZED I HATE WAR AS ONLY A WARRIOR CAN

The news was broadcasting the image of unrest in Turkey[1]. I sat there, watching, as civilians approached an armored vehicle with soldiers standing around it; as the civilians moved forward, the soldiers fired in the air, and I thought to myself, "Dear God, don't let them have to fire on their own people."

I imagined what psychological damage would be done to that soldier if he were to have to fire on his own people. What psychological damage would be done to the one ordering the soldier to fire, the psychological damage done to those who witnessed the act. That is the cost of war. Ricochets of psychological bullets that echo throughout the lives of those who experience it.

Anger built up inside of me, and revulsion, which was a new sensation. That's when I realized: I hate war.

This is not a protest against any particular war; I'm not opposed to our intercession in Iraq, or our action in Afghanistan. I believe I have an understanding of those two conflicts that others may not have, if they weren't involved in them. I'm also not saying that only those of us who fought are allowed to have an opinion about them either; I'm just saying that I hate war, because I know it for what it is, knowledge earned by direct experience.

I know, hate's a strong word. But it's the one I'm using. I don't hate combat, which is a smaller concept than war, but I hate war itself. Combat, an individual firefight, is a reaction to a situation within the war itself; movement to contact, attacking something, defending something. Combat in a firefight is the proper execution of skills learned, or skills developed on the spot; combat is watching the back of your brother and sister. Combat is a skill that is necessary, and the warrior develops skill in combat in order to survive in war and complete the mission…but combat is not war.

I hate war because I understand it, fully and completely, as only one who has experienced it can.

Those who have not directly experienced war can hardly understand what a full sensory experience it is. If you're watching a documentary about combat, you may be able to understand what it looks like, and what it sounds like, even though the vision is two-dimensional and the sound is flat; you don't know what it smells like, though. Sweat, and carbon. The smell of things that burn and fizzle. Watching a documentary doesn't give you the tactile sensation of war, of your shirt sticking to the small of your back or the sting of sweat in your eyes. Or the taste…the bitter taste of fear, the grit of the dirt of whatever country you're operating out of.

Watching a documentary, or even reading an account of war, like this one, doesn't even begin to express the emotions. You may be able to recognize emotions in the face of the warriors in the documentary, but chances are you're not entirely accurate…what seems to be joy or pleasure, to you, might truly cover real fear. What appears to be courage is a snap judgment in a stressful situation.

I think it may be easy to hate war if you've never experienced it, just as it is easy to love war if you've never experienced it.

Mostly, I hate war because I see nearly daily what happens when war ends. The warrior returns from the war, but the battles still rage inside their head. I see veterans shudder and shake when reflecting on those times, shadows and echoes of the emotions they experienced running across their faces. I see veterans who want to scream and rage, but can't. I see veterans who don't want to scream and rage, but do. Mostly, though, I'm tired of death. I'm tired of hearing of more veterans losing their lives, either by their own hand or by the hands of others. I'm tired of the casualties continuing to mount, months and years after the warrior has returned and the guns have gone silent. They never truly do, not in the mind of the warrior.

My wife hates war as only the spouse of a warrior can. She has seen the impact of those times, heard the echoes of war when I sleep. In more difficult times, before getting help, she understood the impact of war even before I did. She does not share my nostalgia about those times, and often does not understand when I say that I miss it…because I miss war, too, as only a warrior can.

I had the opportunity to avoid war, once. Leaving Germany in 2002, I was trying to volunteer to go to the 101st Airborne Division, fully knowing what I was getting myself into, what I was volunteering for. I was practically begging to be sent to war. I had been training and preparing for nearly ten years at that point, but the Army had other plans; I was sent for a three-year tour on Recruiting Duty. In 2005, I was offered the opportunity to remain on Recruiting Duty for the rest of my career, no deployments, no war. I turned it down.

"It's not glorious, you know," a good friend told me. He had served in the Gulf War, and understood where I was coming from, and where I was going. "You want to lead Soldiers in battle, I get it, but you don't understand. Not really."

He was right. And I would say his words to anyone who is envious of a combat veteran now. We can imagine the glory of storming the beaches at

Iwo Jima or Normandy, or standing on the ground of COP Keating, but imagining in no way does it justice.

I hate war because it took very good people away.

I hate war because it continues to take very good people away.

Although I hate war, however, I still believe Thomas Paine's words: "If there must be trouble, let it be in my day, that my child may have peace."

Notes

The Mission Is the Welfare of The Soldier
1. The Army's NCO Creed can be found at https://www.army.mil/values/nco.html

A Veteran Named Skip and His Struggle With PTSD
1. Mikaelian, Allen; Wallace, Mike. (2003). *Medal of Honor: Profiles of America's Military Heroes from the Civil War to the Present.* Hachette Books.
2. The story of Dwight Johnson can be found in a digitized archive of the news article From Dakto to Detroit: Death of a Troubled Hero , May 25th, 1971 https://www.nytimes.com/1971/05/26/archives/from-dakto-to-detroit-death-of-a-troubled-hero-from-dakto-to.html

We Lost Another Veteran Yesterday
1. #22Kill is a nonprofit that aims to create a community that raises awareness and combat suicide by empowering veterans, first responders, and their families through traditional and non-traditional therapies. Find out more at www.22kill.com
2. Iraq and Afghanistan Veterans of America is a veterans advocacy and support organization that supports advocacy, public awareness, and case management support www.iava.org
3. Objective Zero is a mobile app and 501(C)3 Nonprofit that anonymously connects users to a nationwide network of peer support and wellness resources, tools, and training.

A Message from A Veteran to Veterans: You Have the Potential to Change the World
1. Brokaw, Tom (2001). *The Greatest Generation.* Random House Trade Paperbacks.

Lessons from A Pow on Resilience, Perseverance, And Veteran Mental Health
1. Hillenbrand, Laura. (2010). *Unbroken: A World War II Story of Survival, Resilience, and Redemption.* Random House.
2. Vietnam Veteran Paul Dillon appeared on the SuccessVets Podcast on 27 June, 2016 https://www.successvets.com/2016/06/27/paul-dillon-vietnam-vet-goes-into-consulting-entrepreneurship-and-pts-care/

View of A Veteran: I'm No Hero, And I'm Not Special
1. All American Week is an annual reunion of former Paratroopers who served in the 82nd Airborne Division. It is a week that is marked with numerous different activities, including parachute jump demonstrations. To find out more, go to http://www.82ndairborneassociation.org/aaw.html
2. U.S. Census Bureau https://factfinder.census.gov/faces/tableservices/jsf/pages/productview.xhtml?src=CF
3. Frankl, V. E. (1985). Man's search for meaning. Simon and Schuster.
4. Paramount Pictures and Icon Productions present an Icon/Wheelhouse Entertainment production, a Randall Wallace film ; producers, Bruce Davey, Stephen McEveety, Randall Wallace ; written for the screen and directed by Randall Wallace. (2002). We were soldiers. Hollywood, Calif. :Paramount

PTSD: What It Is (And What It Isn't)
1. From the American Psychiatric Association: Posttraumatic Stress Disorder is a psychiatric disorder that can occur in people who have experienced or witnessed a traumatic event such as a natural disaster, a serious accident, a terrorist act, war/combat, rape or other violent personal assault. American Psychiatric Association. (2013). What Is Posttraumatic Stress Disorder? Retrieved from APA Web Site: https://www.psychiatry.org/patients-families/ptsd/what-is-ptsd
2. American Psychiatric Association. (2013). *Diagnostic and statistical manual of mental disorders (DSM-5®).* American Psychiatric Pub.

The Challenges of Veteran Mental Health: Beyond PTSD and TBI

1. Phineas Gage was a railway construction worker who suffered an accident when an explosion caused a tamping iron to pierce his skull, damaging the frontal lobes of his brain. The accident was not fatal, but resulted in profound personality changes and provided the first indication of the functions of the brain and the result of traumatic brain injury. Macmillan, M. (2002). *An odd kind of fame: Stories of Phineas Gage.* MIT Press.
2. Shay, J. (2010). *Achilles in Vietnam: Combat trauma and the undoing of character.* Simon and Schuster.
3. Litz, B. T., Stein, N., Delaney, E., Lebowitz, L., Nash, W. P., Silva, C., & Maguen, S. (2009). Moral injury and moral repair in war veterans: A preliminary model and intervention strategy. *Clinical psychology review, 29*(8), 695-706.
4. Seligman, M. E. (2006). *Learned optimism: How to change your mind and your life.* Vintage.
5. Maslow, A. H. (1943). A theory of human motivation. *Psychological Review, 50,* 370–396.
6. Ibid

Veterans and Maslow's Hierarchy of Needs
1. Ibid

Helping Veterans Trapped by Their Own Experiences: Learned Helplessness and Veteran Mental Health
1. Ibid
2. Toxic Leadership describes a leader who focuses on short-term achievement and focuses on pleasing superiors while being unconcerned about the welfare of subordinates. They are often seen as arrogant, self-serving, inflexible, and petty. Reed, G. E. (2004). Toxic leadership. *Military review, 84*(4), 67-71.
3. The Battle of Kamdesh was an attack on Combat Outpost Keating in Regional Command East, Afghanistan in 2009. To learn more, the first-hand account of the battle can be found in the book Red Platoon. Reed, G. E. (2004). Toxic leadership. *Military review, 84*(4), 67-71.

Meaning, Purpose, And Veteran Mental Health
1. Junger, S. (2016). *Tribe: On homecoming and belonging.* Twelve.
2. James, W., & Burkhardt, F. H. (1983). The Principles of Psychology, the Works of William James.
3. The Sava River delineates the border between Croatia and Bosnia-Herzegovenia. In 1996, Army Engineers created a floating bridge that resulted in the largest river crossing since World War II. https://www.washingtonpost.com/archive/politics/1996/01/01/army-opens-river-bridge/bbc57477-3aa6-4a3c-8065-3c1b57366180/?noredirect=on&utm_term=.c8fab1fc897c
4. Maginot Line was the French line of defense facing Germany, built in the 1930s. It was a series of over fifty fortresses and blockhouses, bunkers, and rail lines.

Moral Injury: The Impact of Combat on Veteran's Individual Morality
1. Litz, B. T., Lebowitz, L., Gray, M. J., & Nash, W. P. (2017). *Adaptive disclosure: A new treatment for military trauma, loss, and moral injury.* Guilford Publications.

Through the Other Side of The Valley of Death: Veterans and Posttraumatic Growth
1. Nietzsche, F. (2018). *The twilight of the idols.* Jovian Press.
2. Seligman, M. E. (2012). *Flourish: A visionary new understanding of happiness and well-being.* Simon and Schuster.
3. Tedeschi, R. G., Park, C. L., & Calhoun, L. G. (Eds.). (1998). *Posttraumatic growth: Positive changes in the aftermath of crisis.* Routledge.

The Stigma of Veteran Mental Health
1. GAO, *Human Capital: Additional Actions Needed to Enhance DOD's Efforts to Address Mental Health Care Stigma,* GAO-16-404 (Washington, D.C.: Apr. 18, 2016).

Military Veterans and The Doomsday Clock

1. Irvin Yalom is a psychologist and pioneer in the field of existential psychology. Yalom, I. D. (1996). *The Yalom reader: Selections from the work of a master therapist and storyteller.* Basic Books (AZ).

2. https://thebulletin.org/doomsday-clock/

3. Yalom, I. D. (2005). The Schopenhauer cure. New York, NY, US: HarperCollins Publishers.

4. Yalom, I. D. (1989). Love's executioner: And other tales of psychotherapy. New York, NY, US: Basic Books.

5. Ibid

A General's Mission Against Mental Health Stigma Can't Be Done Alone

1. https://www.nytimes.com/2016/10/08/world/africa/donald-bolduc-ptsd.html?mwrsm=LinkedIn

2. PDHRA is the Post-Deployment Health Reassessment. This is a health screening designed to evaluate the health of service members returning from combat. Typically conducted between three to six months after redeployment.

Veterans and The Rubber Bullets of Our Thoughts

1. King, S. (1984). *The Ballad of the Flexible Bullet.* Portland, ME: The Magazine of Fantasy & Science Fiction.

2. The Matrix. Dir. Andy Wachowski and Larry Wachowski. Warner Bros. Pictures, 1999.

Combat: It Was the Best of Times, It Was the Worst of Times

1. According to the National Center for PTSD, a range of 11%-20% of Post 9/11 veterans have PTSD, about 12% of Gulf War veterans, and about a 30% PTSD rate over the lifetime of Vietnam veterans.
https://www.ptsd.va.gov/understand/common/common_veterans.asp

The Guns Do Not Go Silent After Combat…Neither Should Veterans

1. Ibid

The Veteran Divide

1. Yalom, I. D. (2002). The gift of therapy: An open letter to a new generation of therapists and their patients.

For Veterans, Success or Struggle in Transition Can Depend on Mental Health

1. Give An Hour is a 501(c)3 Nonprofit that provides no-cost clinical mental health counseling through a network of volunteer mental health professionals www.giveanhour.org

2. The Soldier's Project is a 501(c)3 Nonprofit that provides no-cost clinical mental health counseling through a series of geographically based chapters that partner with local mental health professionals www.thesoldiersproject.org

3. Vet Centers are community based outpatient counseling centers that provide clinical mental health counseling and case management services.
https://www.vetcenter.va.gov

4. Cohen Veterans Network is a foundation that has opened a series of outpatient mental health clinics around the nation www.cohenveteransnetwork.org

For Veterans, Our Capacity for Stress Is Greater Than We Know

1. Permanent Change of Station. This is the relocation of a service member and their family members to a different duty station. Typically occurs every 3-5 years.

For Veterans, Remembering Our Unwavering Resolve Can Drive Our Success

1. Rifelman's Creed. The Creed of a US Marine, written following the attack on Pearl Harbor www.lejeune.usmc.mil/2dmardiv/aabn/Rifleman.htm

2. Soldier's Creed. Produced by the Warrior Ethos program and approved in 2003. https://www.army.mil/values/soldiers.html

3. Sailor's Creed. Produced in 1993 by the Blue Ribbon Recruit Traning Panel. https://www.navy.mil/navydata/nav_legacy.asp?id=257

4. Airman's Creed. Developed in 2007 by the Chief of Staff of the Air Force. https://www.airforce.com/mission/vision

5. Creed of the United States Coast Guarsdman. Written in 1938 by the Commandant of the Coast Guard. http://www.militaryauthority.com/wiki/military-creeds/coast-guard-creed.html

Two Types of Leadership, And How They Apply to Veteran Mental Health

1. John C. Maxwell is an author, speaker, and faith leader who has written some of the leading books on leadership, such as the *The 21 Irrefutable Laws of Leadership*. Learn more at www.johnmaxwell.com

2. Simon Sinek is an author, speaker, and organizational consultant, and author of *Start With Why*. Learn more at www.simonsinek.com

The Strength to Bear Evil: Lessons to A Veteran from Tolstoy

1. Tolstoy, L. (2017). *The forged coupon.* Jovian Press.

2. Warren Corson III is an author and clinical mental health counselor practicing in Connecticut. The blog mentioned is *A Message to Family and Friends of Clinicians*. https://www.counseling.org/news/aca-blogs/aca-member-blogs/aca-member-blogs/2015/09/14/a-message-to-family-and-friends-of-clinicians

3. *Green Mile.* Dir. Frank Darabont. Warner Home Video, 2000. DVD.

The Joy of a Good Plan Well Executed

1. Holcom, R. (Director). (1983). *The A_Team* [Television series]. Hollywood, CA: NBC.

Military Transition: Jumping Out of a Plane in The Fog

1. AWADS is a system of self-contained aircraft instrumentation that delivers personnel, equipment, and supplies during adverse weather.

2. The Department of Defense Transition Assistance Program provides information, access to important documents, and training to ensure separating service members are prepared for post-military life. https://myarmybenefits.us.army.mil/Benefit-Library/Federal-Benefits/Transition-Assistance-Program-(TAP)

Compliment or Criticism, Kevlar Or Velcro?

1. Kevlar is a heat-resistant synthetic fiber that is used for bulletproof materials for service members.

2. 100MPH Tape is a form of military-grade duct tape, with strong adhesive and fiber threads.

Living Life Looking Through A Veteran Filter

1. Controlled Det is short for Controlled Detonation, a controlled explosion used as a method of detonating or disabling a suspected explosive device.

For Veterans, A Rest Plan Is Critical to Future Success

1. Lister Bag: A canvas water bag that hangs from a tripod and is used to deliver chemically purified drinking water to service members.

2. Water Buffalo: A 400 gallon water tank trailer

3. Hippo: The Load Handling System Compatible Water Tank, a 2,000 gallon water tank.

4. Jumpmasters are paratroopers who train and teach military techniques for jumping from airplanes. They are responsible for the supervision, safety, and execution of airborne operations.

5. Charge of Quarters (CQ) is a tasked duty in which a service member is required to be present at the entrance of the barracks. Typically a 24-hour duty performed by two individuals.

Veterans and The Destructive Power of Explosives

1. The M19A1 Claymore mine is a directional anti-personnel mine.

2. The AT-4 is an unguided, portable, single-shot recoilless smoothbore rocket.

The Fallibility...And Humanity...Of Veterans

1. In 1968, a company of American Soldiers brutally killed most of the unarmed

inhabitants of a village, including women, children, and the elderly.

2. Abu Ghraib was a detention center in Iraq that housed detainees from 2003 to 2006. A series of human rights violations, which included physical and sexual abuse, torture, rape, sodomy, and murder, were perpetrated by military and intelligence agency personnel.

3. Cox, M. (2017, May). *Army Investigating 'We Were Soldiers' Legend for Inflating Awards.* Retrieved from Military.com: https://www.military.com/daily-news/2016/05/17/army-investigating-we-were-soldiers-legend-for-inflating-award.html

4. Ibid

5. Cyril Richard Rescorla was a military officer, police officer, and private security specialist. He served in the Ia Drang campaign in Vietnam. On 9/11, he was serving as the head of security for Morgan Stanley, and is credited with saving the lives of over a thousand employees through his preparation and leadership during the crisis. He was one of the few in the company who died on 9/11. He was last seen on the 10th floor, going upwards, just before the South Tower collapsed.

The Things They Carry Now

1. O'brien, T. (2009). *The things they carried.* Houghton Mifflin Harcourt.

Correlation and Causation: Military Service and Killing Machines

1. On July 7th, 2016, an Army Reservist opened fire on a group of police officers in Dallas, Tx, killing five and injuring 9.

2. Correlation and causation are statistical terms that are used to draw conclusions about the impact of events. Correlation tells us how strongly two things are linked and changed together. Causation indicates how one thing will cause the change in another.

3. The Army Marksmanship Unit is a special unit that provides small arms marksmanship training and performs in international shooting competitions.

V Is for Veteran, Not Villain, Victim, Or Vindicator

1. On July 17th, 2016, a Marine Corps data networks specialist opened fire on a group of police officers in Baton Rouge, LA, killing three and wounding three more.

2. "Recent Police Shootings Draw Attention to Veteran's Mental Health," Spectrum News https://spectrumlocalnews.com/nc/charlotte/news/2016/07/18/recent-police-shootings-bring-veteran-mental-health-to-light

3. "Baton Rouge and Dallas shooters were both veterans," The Seattle Times. https://www.seattletimes.com/nation-world/baton-rouge-and-dallas-shooters-were-both-veterans/

4. "Inside the mind of suspected Baton Rouge shooter," WFAA Channel 8 Texas, https://www.wfaa.com/article/news/health/inside-the-mind-of-suspected-baton-rouge-shooter/276315304

5. "Police Shootings and American Veterans' Mental Health," The Daily Kos, https://www.dailykos.com/stories/2016/7/18/1549303/-Police-Shootings-and-American-Veterans-Mental-Health

6. Charles Whitman was a mass murderer who killed his wife and mother in their homes before opening fire from a tower at the University of Texas at Austin, fatally shooting three on his way up the tower. He randomly fired for 96 minutes from the 28th floor observation deck, killing 11 and wounding 31.

7. John Allen Muhammad was a convicted murderer who led the D.C. Sniper attacks in October of 2002. Along with accomplice Lee Boyd Malvo, the pair killed 10 people over three weeks in October of 2002.

8. Lieutenant Colonel Charles Kettle was presented with the Medal of Honor for his actions near Duc Pho, Vietnam on May 15th, 1967. He was presented the Medal of Honor by President Obama in July, 2016
https://www.army.mil/medalofhonor/kettles/

The Stripes Tell A Story…But Not the Whole Story

1. Overseas Service Bars are embroidered gold bars worn horizontally on the right sleeve of Army dress uniforms. Each bar indicate a six-month period of overseas service.

2. The United States Army's National Training Center is a training area located on Fort Irwin, CA in the Mojave desert.

3. The United States Army's Joint Readiness Training Center is a training area located on Fort Polk, LA.

Oz, The Great and Powerful

1. Baum, L. F. (2008). *The wonderful wizard of Oz.* Oxford Paperbacks.

Zero to Sixty Is Fun, Sixty to Zero Not So Much

1. "Difficult Transitions," The Economist, November 12th, 2014 https://www.economist.com/democracy-in-america/2014/11/12/difficult-transitions

Veterans May Not Have Pictures, But They Certainly Have Memories

1. Jay Fabrizi was a U.S. Army Sergeant First Class serving with the 3rd Squadron, 61st Cavalry Regiment, 4th Brigade Combat Team, 4th Infantry Division, Fort Carson, Colo.; died July 14 in Kunar province, Afghanistan, of wounds sustained when his mounted patrol was attacked by enemy forces using rocket-propelled grenades and small-arms fire.

2. Eduvigues Wolf was a U.S. Army Sergeant serving with the 704th Brigade Support Battalion, 4th Brigade Combat Team, 4th Infantry Division, Fort Carson, Colo.; died Oct. 25 at FOB Bostick, Afghanistan, of wounds sustained when insurgents attacked her vehicle with a rocket-propelled grenade.

Four Lessons Learned from A Latrine Stall in Iraq

1. Ibid

2. Ibid

3. The broken windows theory is a criminological theory that states that removing visible signs of crime can reduce further crime

Four Areas in A Veteran's Life That Require Balance, And How to Achieve It

1. A "rollover" is the description of a vehicle accident in which a vehicle is overturned.

For Veterans, Some Things Can Be Hard to Let Go

1. "4 Marines re-create beach pic taken before they left for Vietnam 50 years ago." Eun Kyung Kim, Today.com, April 26th, 2016.

2. MOS stands for Military Occupational Specialty Code, a nine-character code used by the Army and Marine Corps to identify a specific job in the service.

Am I Doing This Wrong? A Veteran's Question

1. Ibid

The Moment I Realized I Hate War as Only A Warrior Can

1. In July of 2016, an attempted *coup d'état was attempted in Turkey against the government of Recep Erdogan. Much of the unrest was broadcast in real time by news agencies around the world.*

ABOUT THE AUTHOR

Duane France is a retired U.S. Army Noncommissioned Officer, combat veteran, and clinical mental health counselor practicing in Colorado Springs, Colorado. In addition to his clinical work, he also writes and speaks about veteran mental health to a wide audience through his podcast and blog, Head Space and Timing, which can be found at www.veteranmentalhealth.com

Made in the USA
Middletown, DE
09 October 2023

40471066R00092